SONGS TO HER GOD

Dear Chad,

I'd like you to
have this.

Thanks for your
friendship & my wishes
to you for future
blessings,

Vicki Chen

12/94

SONGS TO HER GOD

Spirituality of Ann Griffiths

A. M. ALLCHIN

COWLEY PUBLICATIONS
CAMBRIDGE, MASSACHUSETTS

© 1987 by University of Wales and the Welsh Arts Council
All rights reserved.
Published in the United States of America by Cowley
Publications.
International Standard Book No.: 0–936384–53–0
Cover design by Sylvia Slayton

We gratefully acknowledge the permission of the University Press, University of Wales to print a new edition of *Ann Griffiths: The Furnace and the Fountain*, and of Mrs. Vera Hodges to use the translations of Ann Griffiths' hymns by H.A. Hodges.

Library of Congress Cataloging-in-Publication Data
Allchin, A.M.
Songs to her God.
Bibliography: p.
Includes index.
1. Griffiths, Ann, 1776–1805—Religion. 2. Griffiths, Ann
1776–1805—Criticism and interpretation.
3. Christianity in literature. 4. Hymns, Welsh—Texts.
I. Title.
PB2297.G7Z58 1987 891.6'612 87–22155
ISBN 0–936384–53–0

Cowley Publications
980 Memorial Drive
Cambridge, MA 02138

Foreword

The clarion voice of Ann Griffiths, Welsh poet, mystic, and theologian, rings throughout this publication in English of her writings. Long famous in Welsh literature, the treasures of Ann Griffiths' small extant literary corpus—thirty hymns and eight letters—are here presented and illuminated by A.M. Allchin's appreciation of her life, theological vision, and abundant spiritual gifts.

The details of her life are few and unremarkable. Ann Griffiths, who lived from 1776 until 1805, was the daughter of a small landowner and farmer and grew up on a hill farm in mid-Wales. Raised an Anglican in the Church of Wales, she converted in her mid-twenties to Methodism, married a neighboring farmer, and died shortly after the birth and subsequent death of her first child. Yet the literary witness of her life after her conversion to Methodism, which we know largely through her letters and from hymns written down by her contemporaries, are remarkable for their power at once personal and profound.

She speaks with the freshness of a new believer, knitting the commonplace and the eternal into patterns of understanding. Like generations of mystics before her, Ann Griffiths rediscovers God through her own experiences. Her letters provide an extraordinarily clear record of a pilgrim longing to know God throughout the inner trials and daily experiences of the journey. Her hymns are inviting and clear paradigms of prayer and praise; her images, whether bold or subtle, are immediately accessible. There is a theological richness to Ann's spiritual vision—as, for example, an Anglican wonder in the power of the Incarnation fuses with an evangelical longing for eternity.

Ann Griffiths' writings deserve to be known as a "classic" of Christian spirituality, along with the writings of Hildegard of Bingen, Julian of Norwich, and more recently, Simone Weil. In the voices of these formative writers on the spiritual life we are finding, as if for the first time, the power of women's spiritual gifts that have been there for us to discover all along.

Her life and work are important as well because of her very obscurity. To try to understand the witness of a woman who may well be representative of her time and place, the agrarian class of rural Wales in the late eighteenth century, enriches our perception of the actual historical experiences of "common" Christian women. Ann bespeaks the power of the Spirit, the urgency to know Christ, that prevailed among generations of women drawn to the Evangelical revivals of the late eighteenth and early nineteenth centuries throughout the British Isles and America. Ann Griffiths' Welsh testimonies should be compared to those of her Anglo-American contemporaries participating in revival movements, the women of the "burnt- over" district; the analogy would be not only favorable, but revealing. Her example also signifies the need of paying more attention in women's studies to the literary genre of hymnody.

Ann Griffiths is a welcome companion of the spirit. Her witness deserves further scholarly attention, while her testimony had the force and staying power to invite new admirers.

Fredrica Harris Thompsett
Episcopal Divinity School

CONTENTS

ONE

The name of Ann Griffiths is scarcely known beyond Welsh-speaking Wales. Because Ann thought and spoke and sang and wrote in Welsh, her fame until quite recently has been limited to her compatriots. The fact that the island of Britain contains three nations, not one, is itself a surprise to very many people. But the Scots and the Welsh, though much less numerous than the English, have for fourteen hundred years refused to learn the language of their nearest Western neighbours. As a result the riches of Welsh literature, one of the oldest literary traditions of Europe and going back unbroken to the sixth century, remain till today almost wholly unknown throughout the English-speaking world.

In her own idiom Ann's position is universally acknowledged: she is the greatest woman poet to have written in Welsh, and one of the greatest hymn writers in a tradition which is exceptionally rich in hymnody. Even in translation something of the strength and vigour of her hymns becomes apparent. In the last hundred years her work, though small in quantity, has attracted the attention of a large number of writers in Welsh, philosophers as well as theologians, literary critics as well as preachers. She has been the subject of plays and poems; at least one historical novel has been written about her; just this year a film about her life has been made

1

for presentation on Welsh- language TV.

The ecumenical significance of her work, moreover, has become increasingly evident in recent years. Roman Catholics, Non-Conformists, and Anglicans, agnostics as well as evangelicals, have all been attracted to it. So it begins to look as though Ann Griffiths may be one of those figures from the past — Julian of Norwich is a better-known example — who speak more directly to subsequent ages than they did to their own.

Yet if she is to be heard and understood in our late twentieth century, we need to understand something about the language and culture in which she wrote. The contempt in which the Welsh language has been held by the English for centuries has at times affected the Welsh themselves, making them uncertain and defensive about their language and culture. If Welsh was sometimes called the 'language of heaven,' it was more often thought of as the 'language of the kitchen'; the way to advancement in the world was through the acquisition of correct, standard English. Yet in the last thirty or forty years this situation is beginning to alter. Something is happening in Britain that is not unlike the discovery in North America of the culture and tradition of the American Indian peoples. Britain too has its ancient indigenous peoples in the Celts, nations with their own language, culture, their own vision of God, humanity, and the world. What has been despised or ignored for centuries begins to be appreciated in a new way. Hidden and hitherto unsuspected treasures come to light.

It is true that the Welsh language, like other Celtic languages — Breton and Irish and Scots Gaelic — has been

2

pushed to the point of extinction. There are now only about half a million people who have it as their first language. But anyone who begins to learn Welsh discovers in the literature of Welsh Wales a vitality and a resilience which is truly astonishing. The twentieth century in particular has seen a great flowering of poetry in Welsh, and among the poets there have been a number of deeply committed Christians, for example, Gwenallt, Waldo Williams, Saunders Lewis, Euros Bowen, Bobi Jones. In a great variety of ways these poets have affirmed a powerful Christian vision of the world.

In the same way, the whole thrust of Ann Griffith's work is religious rather than national. She deals with universal themes — salvation from death and meaninglessness and sin — in terms of classic Christian tradition of faith and experience. If Ann speaks on behalf of the people of small and forgotten nations, that is in one sense accidental. What is nearer to the heart of the matter is that she speaks on behalf of that great and forgotten multitude, the ordinary men and women who throughout the Church's history have never had the status conferred by education and ordination. Living unrecognised and unknown, outwardly indistinguishable from their neighbours, such people have at times penetrated deeply to the things of God, living lives that were full of the knowledge of eternal life. Ann passed her brief life in a little farmhouse in mid-Wales, a house and place every bit as unremarkable as that of the family at Nazareth.

As we shall see, Ann was a person of some standing in her own community, yet she would hardly have been visible in the society of Regency England. What would the heroines of Jane Austen's novels have made of this uneducated young woman, daughter of a tenant farmer in the remote Welsh hills, who did not even speak English? The quality of Ann's vision as we find it in her hymns and letters not only exposes the blindness of such snobbery, it also places a large question mark against our assumptions about the necessity of formal schooling for the development of the human mind. It is not that Ann was unread. She has an astonishing knowledge of the Bible and a familiarity with much of the Book of Common Prayer. In addition to these she had come to know at least one or two of the classical works of seventeenth-century English divinity, Puritan and Anglican, which were available to her in Welsh translation. Yet Ann had never been to school in any establishment that the authorities would have recognised, then or now; she had no diplomas in theology or in any other subject. So in the end her ability to speak of the things of God with an authority that seizes our attention comes not from books, but from her own experience, from a direct intuition into the mystery of God and his revelation of himself in Christ. Hers was a knowledge received through prayer and sacrament, through faith and obedience, in the silence of prayer and adoration.

'O to penetrate into the knowledge of the one true and living God, to such a degree as might be death to imaginings of every kind . . .' she prays in one of her hymns. It was a prayer that did not go unanswered.

All this may be perplexing to the experts, who are tempted to assume that such utterances as Ann's can only come after a regular initiation into academic disciplines. In her case it is fascinating to see the recurrence of themes and images common enough in patristic theology, but which she can hardly have come across in her very limited reading. The Christian mind and understanding may be renewed from within — dare we say, from above — without there necessarily being direct connections across the centuries. As an eminent French theologian in the earlier part of this century declared of the Carmelite nun, Elizabeth of the Trinity, who died a hundred years after Ann, 'That a young woman of twenty-three or twenty-four attained such an understanding of the word of God as to expound the mystery of grace with such faultless orthodoxy can only be explained by a deep affinity of the soul with it. To speak as she did on such subjects, she must have experienced them directly'. What is true of the Carmelite of Dijon is every bit as true of the farmer's daughter of the Berwyns.

Such a power of visionary understanding as we find in Ann seems to spring from a peculiar fusion of love and knowledge. Yet it is not, as in the arts, primarily a matter of the creative power of the imagination. Ann, like the earlier writers of the Christian tradition, is suspicious of the imagination and asks to be free of 'imaginings' in order to be able to look directly into the revealed mystery of God's love. Rather it is a matter of the development of the receptive, contemplative potential of the human heart and mind, particularly when they are united in one.

Whether this capacity is inherently 'feminine' rather than 'masculine' is a question that needs further investigation; certainly in our society it seems to flourish more among women. Yet that might be a result of the predominately activist and aggressive temper of our age, which tends to attract and affect men more than it does women and certainly inhibits the

5

growth of the contemplative side of human nature. In other societies and other ages, where such capacities have been more valued and better understood, their exercise seems to be more widespread and more evenly distributed between men and women. Perhaps it would be right to think of such a potential for vision and intuitive understanding as something distinctly and profoundly *human*. If this is the case, then it suggests that women have a special role to play in liberating this frozen potential in our society and thus helping to right the disastrous imbalance between contemplation and action that so marks our late twentieth-century civilisation.

Ann Griffiths lived at a time before the more extreme manifestations of this activism had revealed themselves, and in a region that in many ways lived by the rhythms of earlier centuries. As I will seek to show, she was a mystic and theologian of uncommon power, one who saw deeply into the things of God and declared what she saw in memorable words. She is one whose name deserves to have a permanent place not only in the history of her own country, Wales, but throughout the world. Ann speaks of the mystery of Christ and the depths of God's love as things which we can know and enter into here and now. At times she knew God's grace as a consuming fire, at others as a cleansing, healing stream. 'Thanks always', she writes, 'that the furnace and the fountain are so close together'. She opens up dimensions of existence, human and divine, of which we are often almost unaware.

Saunders Lewis, the greatest Welsh writer of this century, has spoken of the crisis of our times as a crisis of meaninglessness rather than of guilt. Faced with the horrors of Auschwitz and Buchenwald, with the threat of nuclear destruction, we ask whether life can have any meaning at all. To such a question Ann replies with her whole being. Her whole life has become an act of worship. 'Ann is a poet', he writes,'putting off her shoes from her feet, because the ground on which she stands at Llanfihangel-yng-Ngwynfa is holy ground. Where there is an object of worship, there cannot be a moment's doubt that life has an eternal meaning, that meaning is everywhere in the universe, and *Y greadigaeth ynddo'n symud* (all creation is moving in him).' So from this life, outwardly so narrow, from this work so apparently in-significant — all we have of hers are some thirty hymns and eight letters — something of incalculable value is given. We find here such a quality of vision, such an exploration of the heights and depths of human experience, such a statement of the central affirmations of the Christian faith, as to make of these things a precious element not only in the tradition of these islands but of the whole of humankind; a kind of focal point in which many things from far and near are gathered. Something has happened in the little house at Dolwar Fach in the parish of Llanfihangel-yng-Ngwynfa which makes of that place a spot memorable for more than one age and for more than one people.

TWO

Ann Griffiths was born in 1776 and died in August 1805 at the age of twenty nine. Her father, John Evan Thomas, who had died in 1804 was a tenant farmer of some standing in his local community, who had more than once been church-warden. Her mother, Jane Thomas, died in 1794 when Ann was eighteen, and since both her elder sisters were already married, Ann from that time on became mistress of the household and remained so until her death. It was a hospitable household, not without its social life. In her early years Ann had the reputation of being a great one for parties, and she loved dancing. As far as travelling is concerned we know that she frequently went to the nearest market town, Llanfyllin, about six miles distant to the east, and that after her conversion she went as often as possible on the monthly Communion Sundays to Bala, twenty-two miles over the Berwyn hills, to hear Thomas Charles preach and to receive the sacrament at his hands. As to further journeys we know nothing. Ann, who uses the image of the sea with such effect, had probably never seen the sea.

The little house where she lived, Dolwar Fach, stands about two and a half miles south of Llanfihangel-yng-Ngwynfa and a little over one mile north of the hamlet of Dolanog, where there is now an Ann Griffiths Memorial

Chapel. It is an isolated farmhouse, in the countryside of steep hills and swift streams, good land but not easy, lying between the barren uplands of the Berwyns to the north and the gentler valley pastures around places like Meifod and Llanfair Caereinion to the south. It was a working farm in the eighteenth century, and is still a working farm today. The family which lives there now is the same family which took over the tenancy in 1806, the year after Ann's death. They are much aware of the fact that their house is also a place of pilgrimage, and are wonderfully welcoming to those who come to visit it. In Ann's day this part of Montgomeryshire was well known for its ballads and folk-songs, its carols and interludes. Bala was a centre for local festivals of poetry and singing; a particularly notable *eisteddfod* of this kind took place in 1789, when Ann would have been thirteen. Composing verses for special occasions is a much commoner accomplishment in Welsh-speaking Wales than it is in England or Scotland. Ann's father had a certain skill in this. All this forms part of the background to Ann's life in the years before her conversion.

Bala was not only a centre for music and versifying. It was also the commercial centre for a cottage industry which flourished in the district — knitting stockings. Life on the land was hard, the small hill farms gave the bare minimum for survival, a bad harvest could bring destitution to a family. It was under these conditions that the lively and imaginative inhabitants gave themselves over to the knitting of woolen stockings. In the months from September to March, whole families would come together at chosen farmhouses (this saved money on candles) in order to knit. Their entertainers at these gatherings were local harpists, storytellers, and poets.

We do not hear of gatherings of this sort taking place at Dolwar Fach, though they may well have done so, but we do know that the family there occupied itself on winter evenings with knitting and weaving, while singing hymns and carols. One of Ann's traits which was remembered after her death was her habit of knitting stockings as presents for impoverished Methodist preachers.

In her lifetime Ann was to be touched by the three major religious influences active at that time in rural Wales — first the Church of England, then the 'old Dissenters' with their roots in the seventeenth century, and finally the new movement of the Methodist revival. She grew up in the parish church at Llanfihangel-yng-Ngwynfa and became familiar there with the prayers and praises of the *Llyfr Gweddi Gyffredin*, the Welsh translation of the Book of Common Prayer. Although she went beyond this tradition after her conversion, that was the church in which she was married, and it is there that she lies buried. At a crucial moment in her life she was greatly influenced by the Independents (Congregationalists) and she remained in contact with their chapel at Llanfyllin till the end of her life. But it was with the Methodists that she found her home. Thomas Charles was the preacher she valued most, and John Hughes the friend to whom she confided her inmost hopes and fears. It is interesting that in our own century she has attracted the attention of Christians of every major denomination, not least Roman Catholic, who have seen in her many of the qualities to be found in their own contemplative saints.

We do not know exactly when the influence of Methodism first began to touch the family at Dolwar Fach. But by 1796 her elder brother John and her younger brother Edward were both deeply involved in the movement; Ann's own conversion probably dates from the following year. From that time onwards, the family which had been deeply attached to the parish church became more and more identified with the Methodist cause. When after her father's death, Ann married, naturally enough she chose a leading local Methodist, Thomas Griffiths, a farmer of Meifod. So Nansi Thomas became Mrs Ann Griffiths, acquiring the name by which she has always since been known. Less than a year later she died, two weeks after the birth and death of her only child Elizabeth. She was buried in the churchyard at Llanfihangel on 12 August 1805.

Ann's life can only be understood against the background of the great evangelical movement of the eighteenth century, which in Wales took the form of Calvinistic Methodism. The movements in England and Wales were closely linked but in many ways independent of one another. Both however, took their origin towards the end of the first half of the eighteenth century.

In Wales during the first generation the main centres of the movement were in the south. The three outstanding figures were Daniel Rowland of Llangeitho (1713-90), William Williams Pantycelyn (1717-91), and Howell Harris (1714-73) whose name is linked with the community of Trefeca. It was only during the second generation, roughly from 1780 to 1810, the period covering Ann's life, that its influence began to be strongly felt in the north. Here the outstanding personality was Thomas Charles of Bala, a man who had been ordained in the Church of England, but who now ministered in his own private chapel. Although the Methodists already formed a world of their own, the decisive split with the Church of England had not yet taken place in Wales at this time. This was to come in 1811, when for the first time the Welsh Methodists ordained their own ministers. Charles was a considerable preacher and a man of some learning. He was a man of more than local reputation, whose name is linked with the founding of the British and Foreign Bible Society. The large Bible Dictionary which he published in the year of Ann's death tells us much of how the Bible was studied and interpreted in the circles where he taught, and helps us to understand the way in which Ann interprets the Old Testament in the light of the New, constantly seeing the person of Christ in the pages of the prophets and the psalms.

In England as in Wales, in all its different forms, Wesleyan as well as Calvinist, within the Church of England as well as outside it, the evangelical movement was one of an intense religious fervour. Its whole aim was to bring men and women to a saving knowledge of God. But as sometimes happens in church history — we may think of the early years of Franciscanism — what begins as a revival of a purely religious nature soon gives rise to an interest in things of a more intellectual kind. It was so here. The part played by the Methodist revival in creating a large and serious minded body of readers in Welsh is familiar to all who care about the Welsh language. It is one of the major factors in the cultural history of Wales during the last two centuries. People had to learn to read and write in order to be able to read the Scriptures, to come to a first hand knowledge of the Word of God. They did so in their own language. Having done that, they wanted to go further and to learn Greek and Hebrew in order to read the texts in the original. And they did this, too. Under the impulse of an awakening of faith and devotion an intellectual awakening took place, which caused farmers and housewives, shopkeepers and shepherds to ponder long and deeply on the ultimate issues of human life. Education and learning were valued among working people in nineteenth-century Wales to a degree that might surprise us today. None of this is irrelevant to a consideration of Ann, for in her writings we shall find a remarkable fusion of intellect and feeling, of love and knowledge. No one could question the reality of the fervour; perhaps it is the intellectual power and clarity which strike us more.

Another of the characteristics of such a movement is that while it has a powerful personal and inward dimension, it grows out of intense shared experience. The power which this corporate enthusiasm can engender in its early stages has a remarkable way of expanding men's and women's vision and their capacity for action. Consider for a moment the little Methodist meeting, of which Ann was a member, at Pontrobert. It contained three Johns, all men of character and initiative. There was first John Thomas, Ann's elder brother, the first of his family to be caught up into the movement and who gradually brought the others into it after him. There was John Davies, a young man who, hearing the call to be a missionary, went with the London Missionary Society to Tahiti and spent the rest of his life there. Finally there was

13

John Hughes, a weaver's apprentice, who became first of all a teacher and eventually a minister. It was he who was Ann's closest friend and advisor in spiritual matters, the recipient of her letters, who married her companion, Ruth Evans, and took down the words of Ann's hymns. If in Ann we find a quality of faith and vision which is in some way unique, we must remember that it arises out of the life and experience of a closely knit group of people of very different aptitudes. Aelred Squire, writing of the first generation of leaders of the Cistercian reform in the twelfth century, speaks of his impression of 'having encountered very individual personalities nurtured in a common climate of thought . . . In the presence of these writers one is haunted by a background of so many unknown eyes and faces. There is no way of recovering what all this meant, but it is certainly of more human importance than anything of which books can tell.' It is the same with the early Methodists; the preachers, the teachers, the hymnwriters give voice to the experience of a multitude of hidden men and women. We can gain from such a book as Morris Davie's *Cofiant Ann Griffiths*, published in 1856, some hint of what the shared assumptions and atmosphere of those early times were like. But constantly one is haunted by a background of so many unknown eyes and faces.

Ann's own part in the movement is clear. She gave expression to some of its deepest and most intimate longings, to some of its strongest and most firmly rooted convictions. But how did she find her way into it? The family in which she grew up was one which took its church membership seriously. Daily prayers taken from the Book of Common Prayer were the rule at Dolwar Fach. The family went to church on

Sundays, and when they were unable to go, the dog went just the same. Education was not altogether neglected. Ann had two or three years of schooling with Mrs Owen y Sais at Dolanog. She learned to read and write, and acquired a little colloquial English, but not enough to read books in that language. The writing of the one letter which is preserved in her own hand is beautiful and regular and strangely mature. But it is noticeable that there is scarcely any sign of punctuation. The quiet respectable religion in which she grew up, like the very brief education which she received, had its limitations. In the end it proved to be insufficient. It could not give that personal assurance of salvation which the Methodist preaching offered. First John, then her second brother Edward, then Ann herself, underwent the experience of conversion and identified themselves with the Methodist cause.

In Ann's case the change seems to have begun with a sermon which she heard at Llanfyllin in the summer of 1796. It was a sermon preached in the open air, and arranged by the old established Independent congregation at Capel Pen-dref. The preacher described a seriousness of Christian commitment which Ann did not know, and she was deeply troubled by his message. At Christmas she found herself going to the parish church alone, weeping and discouraged, since both her brothers were going to the Methodist meeting. She arrived very early before the commencement of the special early morning service, known as the *plygain*. Afterwards the vicar invited her to breakfast. We do not know what exactly he then said, but we may gather that he made disparaging remarks about the new movement of religious enthusiasm.

Whatever it was, it profoundly shocked and disgusted Ann. From this moment on there came a decisive break with the parish church, and shortly afterwards she found conversion.

Ann had always been a leader in the circles in which she lived, prominent alike for her high spirits and her abilities. In her earlier days she had not been averse to making fun of her Methodist neighbours. 'There go the pilgrims on their way to Mecca', she would say of them as they set off to go to Communion Sundays at Bala. Now that she had been converted she went on the monthly pilgrimage herself, though she did not cease to be a leader, nor did her high spirits desert her, even if they were expressed in different ways. She took a prominent part in all the doings of the Methodists — entertaining itinerant preachers and attending the meetings of the *seiat*. In her there was found all the fervour of a religious awakening with all the natural zest of a forceful and attractive personality. But there was something more. Although brief in utterance at a prayer meeting, there was a particular urgency in her petitions. Sometimes she was seen in silent tears as she sat at her spinning wheel, the Bible open on the little table beside her. And then it began to be known that she had composed hymn verses, and that there were moments of visitation.

Let us consider the visitations first. Ann was carried away not only into tears, but at times, into moods of overwhelming exultation. At times there seems to have been something like a trance. A number of these incidents have been recorded for us, and sometimes particular hymn verses have been associated with them. But it would certainly be oversimplifying matters to suppose that the hymns were simply 'given' in such moments of ecstatic experience. Some of them seem to be directly related to matters discussed at the meeting of the *seiat*. Others, we feel sure, must have been the result of long reflection. How exactly Ann herself would have thought about them is something of which we cannot be wholly certain. But at least we can guess something of it from the way in which they have come down to us.

THREE

The way in which her writings have come down to us is one of the most remarkable things about Ann Griffiths. It is one of the things which tells us something of the world she lived in and what was taken for granted in it. Almost all that we have in her own hand is the text of the letter written to Elizabeth Evans, and now kept in the National Library at Aberystwyth. The other seven letters which remain exist only in copies made by their recipient, John Hughes. As to the hymns, they have come to us through oral tradition. Ann, it seems, never made a fair copy of them. We know that she sometimes jotted them down on odd scraps of paper, but none of these has been preserved. What we have, again in John Hughes' handwriting, are the words which Ruth, his wife, dictated to him after Ann's death. It was this same Ruth who had been Ann's companion at Dolwar Fach. Being a good singer she had provided the tunes for the words which Ann had composed. Since she herself was unable to write, we may safely trust the accuracy of her memory.

Here is a striking example of the persistence of oral tradition at the beginning of the nineteenth century, and we ought not to underrate its significance. A writer of our own time, J. C. Campbell, remarks on this subject, 'It is always extraordinarily difficult to convey the feeling and atmosphere of a community where oral tradition and the religious sense are still very much alive, to people who have only known the atmosphere of the modern ephemeral, rapidly changing world of industrial civilisation. On the one hand there is a community of independent personalities where memories of men and events are often amazingly long (in the Gaelic-speaking outer Hebrides they go back to Viking times a thousand years ago), and where there is a standardised world where people live in a mental jumble of newspaper headings and news bulletins, forgetting yesterday's as they read and hear today's . . . where memories are so short that men often do not know the names of their grandparents . . .' This contrast is of help to us in approaching the society of which Ann was a part, and gives us a clue to understanding the context in which she composed and the way in which she thought of her verses.

The massive work of Williams Pantycelyn and his contemporaries had established the central place of hymns in the Methodist movement in Wales. But Pantycelyn was a man of formal education, well aware of the hymn writing of his English colleagues and predecessors, familiar alike with Wesley and Watts; a writer moreover of numerous other works both in verse and in prose. These works, theological, historical, and pastoral, make of Pantycelyn a central figure in both the intellectual and the spiritual history of the movement. Ann, however much she may have been influenced by him, can hardly have thought of herself as a hymn-writer of the same kind. Clearly she had no sense of what we should call literary proprietorship. The verses which she was given were given, she believed, not for herself alone, but for all the

19

members of the community to which she belonged. She at once shared them with Ruth, and thus they passed into use in the meetings of their own and neighbouring *seiats*, knowledge of them spreading rather in the way that knowledge of folk-songs spreads, from singer to singer. It is interesting in this connection to note that Ann's lines frequently contain additional syllables, over and above those strictly necessary metrically. This characteristic, which they have in common with many folk-songs made their singing a problem when more regular hymn tunes came to be adopted later in the nineteenth century and caused many alterations to be made in the published versions of them.

It is not being suggested that Ann thought of her hymns simply as a kind of sacred folk-song. It is difficult to suppose that the writer of some of the greatest of her verses did not feel a literary pride in what she had composed, even if her predominant sentiment was one of gratitude for what she had received. There is a depth and order in her writing which speaks of much intellectual effort. As Gerald Brenan remarks in his study of St. John of the Cross, 'there is a density and complexity of allusion in these poems that prove the absurdity of supposing that he was merely an 'inspired' poet who wrote his poems in ecstasies. A long period of preparation, both consious and unconscious, preceded their composition, and if the ease and sureness with which they spring up show that many of them owe their birth to effortless moments, they were no doubt followed by careful correction and adjustments'. Similarly, a preparatory period of reflective thought and meditation may also mark the hymns of Ann Griffiths.

As we shall see, though Ann's formal education was very slight, she had a mind of uncommon capacity. There is an old handwritten book in the National Library at Aberystwyth that evidently belonged to the household at Dolwar Fach, and which contains copies of ballads and poems by local poets. On one page Ann has written a couple of Bible verses in English and then tried out a word or two in that unfamiliar language. One word is 'Incomprehensibility'. We should have known it was Ann, even if she had not signed her name on the page.

One clue to the background of Ann's hymns is to be found in the importance of carol-singing in her district, a practice which persists to this day. The carols were particularly linked with the *plygain*, the early morning service held at Christmas, but they were also sung at other times. This Christmas service was almost certainly a relic of the old pre-Reformation dawn mass of that feast. It is a striking fact that this celebration should have survived all the vicissitudes of the centuries and still be much alive today. The carols carried down into Ann's time something of the popular faith and devotion of the pre- Reformation centuries.

As is the way with such things, these carols were remarkably conservative both in form and in sentiment. They were also one of the few elements in the traditional folk culture of which the new religious movement did not disapprove. So a minor Methodist poet of the 1830's, Dafydd Hughes (1792-1860), *Eos Ial*, could produce carols of a type which might well date from the seventeenth century or earlier, and which make rich use of the Old Testament imagery which Ann employs in her hymns. Here are a few verses of

21

a carol of his still sung today in the Tanant Valley.

Ar gyfer heddiw'r bore, 'n Faban bach,
'n Faban bach,
Y ganwyd gwreiddyn Jese, 'n Faban bach;
Y Cadarn ddaeth o Bosra,
Y Deddfwr gynt ar Seina,
Yr Iawn gaed ar Galfaria, 'n Faban Bach,
'n Faban bach,
Yn Sugno bron Mareia, 'n Faban bach.

Caed bywiol ddwfr Eseciel, ar lin Mair, ar lin Mair,
A gwir Feseia Daniel, ar lin Mair;
Caed bachgen doeth Eseia,
'R addewid roed i Adda,
Yr Alffa a'r Omega, ar lin Mair, ar lin Mair,
Mewn cor ym Methlem Jiwda, ar lin Mair.

Diosgood Crist ei goron, o'i wir fodd, o'i wir fodd,
Er mwyn coroni Seion, o'i wir fodd;
I blygu ei ben dihalog
O dan y goron ddreiniog,
I ddioddef dirmyg llidiog, o'i wir fodd, o'i wir fodd,
Er codi pen yr euog, o'i wir fodd.

Am hyn, bechadur, brysia, fel yr wyt, fel yr wyt,
I'mofyn am y noddfa, fel yr wyt;
I ti'r agorwyd ffynnon
a ylch dy glwyfau duon

22

Fel eira gwyn yn Salmon, fel yr wyt, fel yr wyt;
Gan hynny tyrd yn brydlon, fel yr wyt.

On this day's morn was born a little child,
a little child,
The root of Jesse was born, a little child,
The mighty one of Bozra,
The lawgiver on Mount Sinai,
The atonement won on Calvary, a little child,
a little child,
Sucking at Mary's breast, a little child.

The living waters of Ezekiel, on Mary's knee,
on Mary's knee,
The Daniel's true Messiah, on Mary's knee,
The wise child of Isaiah,
The promise given to Adam,
The Alpha and Omega, on Mary's knee,
on Mary's knee,
In a stall in Bethlehem Judah, on Mary's knee.

Christ put aside his crown, of his free will,
of his free will,
That Zion might be crowned, of his free will,
To bow his undefiled head,
Beneath the thorny crown,
To suffer angry scorn, of his free will,
of his free will,
To raise the guilty's head, of his free will.

23

Hasten to him Sinner, therefore, as you are,
as you are,
To seek in him a refuge, as you are,
For you a well is opened
To wash your wounds, and make you
As pure as snow on Salmon, as you are, as you are,
So come without delaying, as you are.

When we think of the area where Ann grew up as remote,
that may only reflect our own city-centred narrowness. As J.
C. Campbell reminds us, such places are sometimes rich in
an oral culture which conveys to the present values from the
distant past, and brings the world of eternity close to every
day.

Yet while we ought not to ignore the influence of some elements of the popular religion of Ann Griffiths' day, we are on
much surer ground when we come to two books which we
know that she must have constantly used and read — the
Bible and the Book of Common Prayer. It was these two
books which formed her heart and mind, and between them
there can have been no rivalry. It is the Bible which must have
taken first place, with the Prayer Book providing one of the
principal ways by which its teaching was assimilated. We
who are used to a multitude of books and periodicals, let
alone to the bombardment of our senses by radio and
television, can hardly imagine what these books must have
meant in an age where printed matter was hard to come by
and the divine authority and origin of the Scriptures was unquestioned. For Ann, as for Christians through many ages,
the Bible was a whole world, a world in which she found her

own condition mirrored, a world in which God's word was constantly to be heard addressing her.

Moreover, the mode of interpreting the Bible, according to principles that in their main outline go back to the first Christian centuries, enabled the perceptive reader to see a unity in all the different books, which escapes our more historically-conditioned minds. As the seventh of the Thirty- Nine Articles declares — a text with which Ann would have certainly been familiar — 'The Old Testament is not contrary to the New; for both in the Old and New Testament everlasting life is offered to mankind by Christ, who is the only Mediator between God and man, being both God and man'. So in her hymns, which are woven out of a tissue of biblical quotation and allusion, Old Testament types are constantly seen in reference to Christ. It is so, for instance, in one of the most familiar of them, perhaps the one which is most universally loved amongst Welsh-speaking Christians, 'Wele 'n sefyll rhwng y myrtwydd . . . There he stands among the myrtles. . . .' The mysterious figure of the horseman in the prophet Zechariah, who appears with good news for Zion, is at once and without question taken as a type of Christ.

The same process can be seen at work in the way in which Ann handles the stories of the Old Testament. For her, they are not episodes out of a remote past. They speak to her directly of God's dealings with his people, that people to which she herself belongs, and they speak of his mercy and his judgement of nations and individuals now, no less than in the past. She reads with faith and she reads with imagination, and distant incidents come to life with extraordinary vividness. She writes in one of her letters to John Hughes,

I have found much pleasure in meditating on the Shunammite woman who set aside a room on the wall for the man of God to rest in when he passed by, placing in it a bed, a table, a stool and a candlestick. Perhaps that woman, in her longing for the prophet, often paced the room, and found satis faction in watching for the man.

The experience of the woman in Palestine almost three thousand years before, becomes her own experience as she longs for the coming of John Hughes, the one person with whom she can speak altogether freely of spiritual things.

This is not just a sentimental or historical identification with a figure in the past. Through the surface meaning of the Scriptures Ann always sees deeper levels of significance, just as in her own life, the everyday events of life on the farm became the ways by which she entered into contact with eternal realities. She takes it for granted that a sacred text has many levels of interpretation. So the experience of waiting, of feeling the absence of one whose presence is greatly desired, is immediately referred by her to a greater and more universal experience; the situation of the believer when the sense of the Lord's presence is removed, when God makes himself known to us only as a painful absence. The longing for the coming of the man of God is a symbol for the longing for the advent of God himself. And in this predicament 'it comforts the heart of a believer, in the absence of the *visible* countenance of her Lord, that in some sense the furniture is still there'. The furniture, that is to say the words and promises of Scripture, the articles of Christian belief, the common structures of faith and life are still present, even when the Lord seems to have gone.

For we notice here one of the primary characteristics of Ann's mind, its great precision. She speaks of the absence of the visible countenance of the Lord. She knows in her faith that he is not really absent, even when he seems most painfully to be so. So in a few lines, she tells us her experience, places it in a long historical perspective and sees that history itself as pointing to an eternal reality, to an eternal now in which the distance between Shunem and Berwyn suddenly becomes of little significance.

One of the things which would have helped Ann to see the Scriptures in this way, was the fact that since her childhood she had constantly been meeting the texts of the Bible in the context of prayer. For in the Christian tradition, it is believed that it is in prayer that eternity touches time, that we are 'with angels and archangels and all the company of heaven'. The daily prayers at home taken from the Book of Common Prayer, the regular prayer of the parish church, Sunday by Sunday, would have introduced her to this particular way of using the Bible. Long before her conversion, habits of thought and attention were being built up, which later blossomed into her awareness of an eternal now. The word 'today' for instance, used in the phrase 'Today if you will hear this voice', which occurs in the psalm always said at the beginning of Matins, acquires a great wealth of meaning and association, in this way, linking the present moment with an eternal action. But not only in the use of the Bible in worship did the past come forcibly into the present. Still more in the Holy Communion past, present and future were for her united in the coming of the Lord.

It is a noteworthy fact that in eighteenth-century Methodism, in Wales no less than in England, the sacrament of the Eucharist had a vital place. While, in the parish churches of the land, the sacrament was administered infrequently and sometimes with no great reverence, amongst the Methodists there was a real revival of sacramental practice and devotion. At Llangeitho in the south for instance, where for years the preaching of Daniel Rowland attracted crowds from all over Wales, it was the Sacrament Sundays which often saw the largest congregations and the moments of greatest fervour. For the Methodists, both Welsh and English, the Communion was a 'converting ordinance'. On the monument to Howell Harris which is to be found in the parish church at Talgarth, we read, 'Near the Altar lie the remains of Howell Harris Esquire, born at Trevecka, January 23rd, 1713/14 O.S. Here where his body lies, he was convicted of sin, had his pardon sealed, and felt the power of Christ's precious blood, at the Holy Communion'. For people such as these there could be no doubt but that the Sacrament no less than the Word stood at the heart of Christian worship.

In Ann's own life, the monthly journey to Bala on Communion Sundays became a moment of particular significance. Quite a number of the stories which we have about her relate to the expeditions over the mountains, usually in company, occasionally alone. We have a picture of the young people hurrying down the narrow valley towards Bala on the Sunday morning from the inn at Llanwyddyn where they had stopped to spend the night. We hear of the journey in the evening with Ann going over again the points which had been treated in the sermon. One verse of a hymn in particular, is linked with a return journey when Ann was by herself, riding this time, lost in meditation on the things she had heard, the things she herself had shared in.

> Blessed hour of rest eternal,
> Home at last, all labours o'er;
> Sea of wonders never sounded,
> Sea where none can find a shore;
> Access free to dwell for ever
> Yonder with the One in Three;
> Deeps no foot of man can traverse —
> God and Man in unity.

The sacrament of the Eucharist is understood not only as the moment when the Christian looks back to the Last Supper and the act of offering which it initiated. It has also always been seen as a moment of anticipation, a foretaste of the final rejoicing which shall be ours in the kingdom of heaven. The gospels themselves are full of stories of dinner parties and shared meals; the theme of a great and royal banquet recurs frequently in the parables of Jesus. This is how Ann herself found it to be. She has found in the worship she has shared in that Sunday in Bala the promise of a perfect sabbath rest, an entry into the very life of the triune God.

As I have already suggested, Ann sees all this in terms of the classical Christian tradition and expresses what she sees in words of remarkable precision. In this single verse she has referred us to two of the basic articles of the Christian faith,

29

the one in God as Trinity, the other in the union of God with humanity in Christ. Through the Incarnation we are enabled to enter into and share in that sea of wonders, that ocean of joy and love and mutual self-giving, which the tradition has sought to affirm exists in God himself, saying that God is at once three and one. And in this verse, which has sometimes been cited to show that Ann believed in a kind of 'absorption' mysticism, where human being is simply dissolved in God, we find when we look more carefully that she is saying something quite different. In being called to enter into that eternal rejoicing, we do not cease to wonder or to praise; we do not cease to grow in knowledge and in love. Separation is destroyed, but not at the cost of human annihilation. There is abundant freedom of entrance into a life that knows no ending.

How is it that Ann manages in this way to wed depth of feeling to intellectual lucidity? It is not, after all, so easily done. Eccentric figures, intense and sometimes powerful, with their idiosyncratic visions and their individual theories, are not lacking in the history of Christianity, particularly in the history of Protestantism. There is nothing of this in her writing; rather we find a classical balance and sobriety. How is it, again with her sense of being drawn into the very life and being of God, that she does not simply lose herself in 'oceanic feeling', or like Emily Bronte, only a few years later, find herself inventing a private language to express her experience? Where does this element of order and structure come from?

We have already hinted at one of its principal sources in speaking of the Book of Common Prayer. There Ann would have found in texts with which she had long been familiar, the Te Deum, and the Apostles' and the Nicene Creed, for instance, the outlines of that faith which she expounded. In the Athanasian Creed we may suppose that her enquiring mind would have found a particular fascination. What is certain is that her grasp of both Trinitarian and Christological doctrine is remarkably sound, as we see for instance in the verse of the hymn where she speaks of

> Two natures in one Person
> Joined indivisibly,
> True, pure and unconfounded,
> Perfect in unity.

Equally remarkable is her capacity to sum up in a few lines a whole history of Christian teaching and experience. Speaking again of the person of Christ, in the following verse, she says,

> True man, in all thy weakness
> He truly feels for thee;
> True God, o'er world, flesh, Satan
> He reigns victoriously.

When we come to ask in detail how much she might have read, it is very difficult to give a definite answer. Certainly not much in terms of modern reading habits, but perhaps more than we should at first expect. There was quite an amount of theological and spiritual writing available in Welsh in the later eighteenth century. It is more than possible that she could have read, for instance, a translation of Richard Baxter's book *The Saints' Everlasting Rest*. With its fervent meditations on the glory of heaven, there is much in it which would have caught her attention. Again she might have known Bishop William Beveridge's *Particular Thoughts upon Religion*, a work which contains a remarkable clear exposition of the doctrine of the Trinity. In meeting such writers as these she would have been coming into contact with major figures in seventeenth century Anglican and Puritan divinity, and it may be that it was through them that she got something of her own feeling for the shape and quality of Christian doctrine.

Standing behind such writers as these, there were of course the great Christian thinkers of the earliest centuries, whose names we may suppose she hardly knew, who had hammered out in the course of violent controversy the basic outline of the faith which she received through the Creeds and the liturgical formularies. Nearer to her own time, there was another towering figure of a comparable importance, John Calvin. The clarity of his grasp upon the essentials of the Christian faith, the particular emphasis which he laid on belief in the absolute sovereignty and majesty of God and his purposes for humankind from all eternity, are things which had come down to her through the whole weight of the teaching of the movement of which she was a part. Like John Hughes, with whom she doubtless discussed these matters and from whom certainly she learned much, she was altogether ready to receive the great positive affirmations of this most lucid of the sixteenth century reformers. If, as we shall suggest, there are in Ann unexpected themes and emphases which remind us of older traditions of Christian theology than that of Calvin's Geneva, this does not mean that she was not deeply indebted to the stream of teaching which came from him.

This element of almost Gallic clarity in Ann's writing, both in her hymns and her letters, is perhaps one of the things which gives us a clue to understanding her position within the literary tradition of Wales. Ann belongs to that one Celtic nation which in the origins of its language and its literature was deeply touched by the order and discipline of the Roman Empire. In a great variety of ways that Latin influence has continued to be active in the cultural tradition of Wales. We may perhaps see, through Ann's combination of intensity of feeling with clarity of thought, something of that fusion of different elements which has played so great a part in shaping the inheritance of Wales. In her, the experience of the first age of the saints seems to live again. She presents us, in a time not so remote from our own, with a possibility of communion with what is most central and essential in the whole Christian tradition. In other Welsh writers of our own century no less than of hers, we feel a closeness to our origins, and a living contact with those sources of life which too easily are forgotten or obscured today.

FOUR

Let us move now from the discussion of Ann Griffiths'
sources to a consideration of her hymns, and turn first to one
of the best known of them. It is, incidentally, the only one to
have found its way into the hymn-books in something like
the form in which it was first written down; in the case of almost all the others, verses have been rearranged and
amended to suit the taste of generations of editors. Even
here, the more correct word *llywydd* has been substituted for
Ann's anglicism, *beilat*, in the second verse.

> There he stands among the myrtles,
> Worthiest object of my love;
> Yet in part I know his glory
> Towers all earthly things above;
> One glad morning
> I shall see him as he is.

> He's the beauteous Rose of Sharon,
> White and ruddy, fair to see,
> Excellent above ten thousand
> Of the world's prime glories he.
> Friend of sinners,
> He's their pilot on the deep.

What have I to do henceforward
With vain idols of this earth?
Nothing can I find among them
To compete with his high worth.
Be my dwelling
In his love through all my days.

Wele'n sefyll rhwng y myrtwydd
Wrthrych teilwng o fy mryd,
Er mai o ran yr wy'n adnabod
Ei fod uwchlaw gwrthrychau'r byd;
Henffych fore,
Y caf ei weled fel y mae.

Rhosyn Saron yw ei enw,
Gwyn a gwridog, teg o bryd,
Ar ddeng mil y mae'n rhagori,
O wrthrychau penna'r byd;
Ffrind pechadur,
Dyma ei beilat ar y mor.

Beth sy imi mwy a wnelwyf
Ag eilunod gwael y llawr
Tystio'r wyf nad yw eu cwmni
Yw cystadlu a Iesu mawr;
O am aros,
Yn ei gariad ddyddiau foes.

We have already remarked on the way in which the hymn
begins with the figure of one of the angelic messengers of the

Old Testament, and at once identifies him with the Christ, who is at once the messenger and the message from God. The first verse contains at least two further allusions to the Bible, this time to passages in the New Testament. Ann is full of wonder to see amidst the objects of this world one who is above all these objects, one who can command the assent of her whole heart and mind in a way that no created thing can do. Here is all the paradox of the notion of incarnation. God the creator enters into his creation. Her knowledge of him now, she says, must be in part, thus echoing the words of St. Paul at the end of one of the most famous passages in his letters, 'now I know in part, then I shall know even as I am known'. Like St. Paul, this thought leads Ann forward to long for the time when 'that which is perfect is come and that which is in part shall be done away'. (1 Cor. 13, 12). 'Hail to the morning when I shall see him as he is.'

In this last line, however there is also a reminiscence of the first Epistle of St. John. 'Beloved now are we the sons of God, and it doth not yet appear what we shall be; but we know that when he shall appear we shall be like him, for we shall see him as he is.' (1 John 3, 2). This passage, which like the words which have just been quoted from St. Paul, has had an incalculable influence on the development of Christian experience through the ages, shows us again the tension between what is given now and what shall be given hereafter, beyond this world of space and time. This eager expectation, this movement towards the future, is something which Ann knows well. With her, as with all the great contemplatives down the ages, the vision of eternity, granted within the world of time, sets up an intense longing for its fulfillment in a realm beyond this one.

William of St. Thierry in the twelfth century, having spoken so eloquently of the moment of vision, has this to say:

> For nowhere doth the mode of human imperfection become more manifest to itself than in the light of the countenance of God and the glass of divine vision; where in the Day that is, seeing more and more what it lacketh, it amendeth daily by likeness that wherein it faileth by unlikeness. . . . For it is impossible that the Sovereign God should be seen and not loved; or not loved as much as it hath been suffered to be seen; till love advance to some likeness of that love which did make God like to man in the humility of human estate, to the end that He might make man like to God in the glory of the partaking of the divine.

Here too there are echoes of the passage from St. John just noted, which continues, 'And every one that hath this hope purifies himself, even as he is pure'.

This longing to be pure and remain faithful to the vision is one that Ann expresses in the two subsequent verses of the hymn; we shall find it again when we come to look at the contents of her letters. In these verses, after the almost austere statement of the first line (an *object* worthy of my whole *mind*), we come to the more effective language of the Song of Songs, to the vision of the Lord as friend and guide through the perplexities of this life. Mind and heart together are caught up into the vision.

The final verse confronts us sharply with the question of Ann's attitude towards the created world. Are all the things that God has made to be considered simply as idols, things to be rejected? There is no doubt that at times in Christian tradition the movement of turning away from the world to God has been made in a one-sided and exaggerated way. That this was sometimes the case in Wales in the nineteenth century is suggested by the force with which many of the most deeply Christian poets of our own time have stressed the other side of the picture — that God is to be loved in and through all his works, and not apart from or against them. Evidently these poets have felt the need to reply to what seemed to be an unduly negative strain in the spirituality of the previous century.

God has not forbidden us to love the world,
and to love man and all his works. . .

declares Gwenallt in the opening flourish of one of his finest sonnets. And more gently, but no less incisively, Euros Bowen takes this very line of Ann, 'What more have I to do?' and replies to it with the lines

But to compare
beauty
and delight
and majesty
with the poetry
which is in the poor idols of the world.

The point both poets are making is incontrovertible within any whole and balanced Christian view of the world. God is to be loved in all things, as well as above all things. To say anything else would imply a denial of the goodness of what he has made. But in reply to this criticism, which applies of course not only to Ann, but to the whole of the movement of which she was a part, two things need to be said. First, it is clear that Ann's position is not a wholly negative one. She finds all created things of little value, not because she despises them in themselves, but because she has seen something else, a vision of an eternal splendour with which they cannot compare. We may not share her experience, but we can hardly doubt its reality for her, or fail to acknowledge that many bear witness to it through the centuries. When compared with the greatness of God the creator, things of this world suddenly seem trivial; the whole creation is seen as very small, small as a hazel-nut held in the palm of the hand, as Julian of Norwich put it in the fourteenth century. Ann says the same thing in different words,

> Earth cannot, with all its trinkets,
> Slake my longings at this hour;
> They were captured, they were widened
> When my Jesus showed his power.
> None but he can now content me,
> He, the Incomprehensible;
> O to gaze upon his person
> God in man made visible.

But from the Christian point of view there is a second point to be made. To love God above and beyond all the things that he has made need not lead us to despise those things in themselves. Rather, as with Julian of Norwich, it may lead us to regard them as precious and good, despite their limitations and fragility. The movement away from the world to God may be followed by a movement back towards the world, seen now as the object of God's love. There is a dialectical movement here which in the end is essential to the maintenance of the Christian vision of the world as God's word and gift to us. Both sides are necessary. Only if we can see God's glory shining out beyond all things, shall we be able to see that same glory shining out in all things.

How far Ann herself would have been able to make that second step it is impossible to say. There were strands in the teaching of Welsh Methodism — its comparative neglect of the doctrine of creation for instance, and its great stress on human sinfulness and corruption — which would have made it difficult. Ann's unexpected emphasis on the doctrine of our creation in God's image and likeness suggests that she was not altogether unaware of these problems. It is possible too to regard her decision to marry as an expression of a more mature and balanced hold upon the twin ways of affirmation and rejection.

What does seem clear is that in practice, if not in theory, a grasp upon the potentially sacramental nature of the world seems to have been present in many parts of Welsh Nonconformity throughout the nineteenth century. Whether, because life was lived in such close contact with the natural order, or because of an unconscious hold upon earlier traditions, Christian and even pre-Christian, the negative and censorious face of the movement was not by any means always predominant. The society described by D. J. Williams in the first volume of his autobiography, *The Old Farmhouse*, is not a notably life-denying nor outwardly religious one. But when he tells us of his father, 'His great gift was the gift of prayer. It was a joy to listen to him when he knelt', we are made to pause. Still more, when speaking of his mother he confides, 'She was quite selfless and without any desire to be seen. Her treasure was her inward life. . . She did not speak much of her religion beyond praising the goodness she saw in others and being tender towards their weaknesses. . . It is my belief that her life, every minute of it as it came, was all one secret prayer', we recognize at once the world of which Ann's letters speak. There is the same demanding life on a small hill farm, the same realisation of a hidden treasure at the heart of our human life. Something of the experience of the first Methodist generations lived on in the chapel at Rhydcymerau, as in many other places, at the beginnings of our own century and contributed to a life in which grace and nature were at one.

As regards Ann herself, there is much that we cannot know. What we have in her letters and her hymns is the testimony of one who, in her mid-twenties, has looked deeply into the things of eternity and been so dazzled by the splendour of what she has seen that she has no eyes for anything else. Her mind and her affections have alike been captured and enlarged. Nowhere is this combination of intellectual and effective insight more in evidence than in the greatest of her hymns, so striking at once in its content and in its fervour.

As Saunders Lewis says, it is rightly to be regarded as 'one of the majestic songs in the religious poetry of Europe'.

> Wondrous sight for men and angels!
> Wonders, wonders without end!
> He who made, preserves, sustains us,
> He our Ruler and our Friend,
> Here lies cradled in the manger,
> Finds no resting-place on earth,
> Yet the shining hosts of glory
> Throng to worship at his birth.
>
> When thick cloud lies over Sinai,
> And the trumpet's note rings high,
> In Christ the Word I'll pass the barrier,
> Climb, and feast, nor fear to die;
> For in him all fullness dwelleth,
> Fullness to restore our loss;
> He stood forth and made atonement
> Through his offering on the cross.

The first verse begins with an exclamation of wonder, of amazement, before the mystery of the Incarnation. It is very striking and very typical of Ann that she should begin at this point. The whole emphasis of the Evangelical movement, of which Methodism was a part, lay on the problem of human sin and guilt before the righteousness of God. Hence the cardinal point in all evangelical preaching was the doctrine of the Atonement, the explanation of the way in which God's forgiveness comes to sinners through the sacrificial death of

Christ upon the cross. As we shall see, this emphasis is also central for Ann.

Yet she places this problem within the context of a wider, deeper mystery about God's relationship with humanity, one which the Evangelicals never denied, but tended to pass over somewhat rapidly. For her, the basic problem is one of human finitude and God's infinity, and so for her the starting point is the belief that God, who is 'the giver of being, the generous sustainer and ruler of everything that is', has entered into creation and accepted the limitations of our human state, vividly symbolized by the swaddling clothes in which the infant Jesus was wrapped. Thus the doctrine of our redemption is placed within the doctrine of God's Incarnation, God's coming in flesh to be where we are, so that by this gift we may be raised up where he is.

This idea of the believer's ascent to God follows on directly in the second verse of the hymn. How can men and women go up to God? Here we have one of the most remarkable examples of the way in which Ann restates a basic theme of Christian spirituality, which she can hardly have known directly through her reading. The story of Moses going up to speak with God in the cloud on Mount Sinai was taken by the theologians of the early centuries — Gregory of Nyssa, for example — as an image of the way in which the believing heart and mind must approach the presence of the inaccessible God. Only as believers go up through the cloud and the darkness, setting aside their own ideas and concepts, their own images and desires, can they become able to receive the revelation which God wills to give us. No one can see God and live. There is a death to self that is inescapable on

43

this ascent. But in Christ the Word, in whom humanity and God are fully reconciled and at one, this death no longer holds terror for us. Our death is included in his death, our life is united with his triumphant life. In him the barriers erected by sin and the guilt, the barriers of death itself, are taken away.

So we come to the two central verses of the hymn.

He between a pair of robbers
Hung, our Making-good to be;
He gave power to nerve and muscle
When they nailed him to the tree;
He, his Father's law exalting,
Paid our debt and quenched our flame;
Righteousness, in fiery splendour,
Freely pardons in his name.

See, my soul, where our Peace-maker,
King of kings, was lowly laid,
He, creation's life and movement,
Of the grave a tenant made,
Yet on souls fresh life bestowing;
Angels view it with amaze;
God in flesh with us adoring;
Heaven's full chorus shouts his praise.

The Welsh of the first two lines reads, 'Efe yw'r Iawn fu rhwng y lladron,/ Efe ddioddef angau loes', and the more literal translation would read, 'He is the satisfaction that was between the thieves'. The word *iawn* (satisfaction) has a multitude of meanings in Welsh: it means what is right, what is fitting, what is true. In the midst of our human failure, our thievery, our wasting of God's gift, God comes to be in us the reconciliation; to be in that place the new source of goodness and of truth. The paradoxes which are so characteristic of Ann's style are heightened to an ever-increasing degree, and we cannot but think of the verses in the Byzantine rite for Good Friday, though she could have had no knowledge of them:

> He who clothes himself with light as
> with a garment,
> Stands naked at the judgement.
> On his cheek he received blows
> From the hands which he had formed.

Or again

> Today is hanged upon the tree
> He who hanged the earth in the midst
> of the waters.
> A crown of thorns crowns him
> Who is the King of the angels.
> He is wrapped about with the purple of mockery
> Who wraps the heaven in clouds.

The verse that expounds the mystery of the cross leads us on to the lines that set forth the mystery of the tomb, of Christ's descent among the dead. Here Ann gives us what is without any question her most startling image, which sees the creator and redeemer of all lying dead in the tomb, all creation moving in him. Some of the greatest Christian thinkers of our own time, Hans Urs von Balthaser for instance, have underlined the relevance of this particular article of faith for our own age. Christ's descent into the place of death, the place of separation from God, is an element of the Christian tradition which can speak most powerfully to a civilization that has a fearful sense of alienation from the roots of being and of meaning. By taking human alienation and human death into himself, God raises up all of humanity into new possibilities of life.

In this respect, the Eastern Orthodox icon of the resurrection is extremely eloquent. It shows Christ not as a solitary figure rising from the grave, but rather as the victor over death drawn up with Adam and Eve — as the representatives of all men and women. However, Ann's image of the prince of life lying dead in the tomb, the forces of life still latent within him, is an infinitely suggestive one. It gathers together elements from the mythology and poetry of many ages and many people. The sleeping Lord will one day return. But here his awakening has already taken place; life shines forth from the tomb. He who descended is already ascended. The flesh that has been imprisoned is already set free, and before God all the heavenly powers rejoice. Here again, in the juxtaposition of death and resurrection, as well as in the association of human with angelic praise, there are remarkable parallels with the Byzantine hymnody for Holy Week:

I magnify thy sufferings,
I praise thy burial and thy resurrection
Proclaiming, Lord, glory to thee.

What is being said here is that the substance of human existence, both personal and historical (our flesh, the stuff of our life) is not doomed to futility and death. Rather it is lifted up into the infinite possibilities of the eternity of God. The human fear of death, the fear of meaninglessness, is overcome. There is an object of worship, God in flesh; not we alone, but all creation, can enter into union with him.

So the hymn, which up until this moment has been centred upon the mystery of that object, tracing his journey from Bethlehem to the cross, from the empty tomb to the mount of ascension, now takes on a more purely personal, even subjective, tone.

Thanks for ever, thanks ten thousand,
While I've breath, all thanks and praise
To the God who all his wonders
For my worship here displays,
In my nature tried and tempted
Like the meanest of our race,
Man — a weak and helpless infant,
God — of matchless power and grace.

Gone this body of corruption,
'Mid the fiery hosts on high,
Gazing deep into the wonders
Wrought of old on Calvary,

47

God, the Invisible, beholding,
Him who lives, yet once was slain,
Clasped in close eternal union
And communion I'll remain.
There, new-fashioned in his likeness,
Veils and fancies done away,
To the Name by God exalted,
Highest homage I shall pay.
There, communing in the secret
Seen in those deep wounds he bore,
I shall kiss the Son for ever,
Turning from him nevermore.

In a preliminary way we must notice two things. First, Ann is very reticent on the subject of the sufferings of Christ. The absolute centrality of his sacrificial death within the scheme of salvation is never in question in any of her writings. But a detailed and painful meditation on the incidents of the passion, something which had been common enough in the devotional writing of Catholicism and Protestantism alike, is wholly absent from her. It is the simple thought of *'who it is that was on the cross'* which arrests her mind in amazement. That the generosity and love of eternity should be present in, and in some way active through the most sordid, inexplicable elements of human experience, this is what captures her attention as it has done that of Christians throughout the ages. It is this which she points to in speaking of the mystery revealed in the wounds.

Secondly, in reference to the kiss of the last line of all, we must notice that though the words of the Song of Songs seem constantly to be at the back of her mind, she is very sparing in explicit use of the imagery of bride and bridegroom to describe the relationship of the soul with God. In one of her letters she speaks of her longing for a 'marriage union' with God in his Son. In one of her hymns she speaks of the cross as her husband's cross. But that is all. This also is a place where Christian devotion has at times run into strange extravagances. We do not find them in Ann. 'Thanks for ever, thanks ten thousand,/While I've breath, all thanks and praise. . . .' Our power to praise and our capacity to rejoice is set free. With all the powers of heaven we can glorify God and give thanks for the wonder of the Word made flesh. There is a tone of ecstasy in verses five and six. Again the play of paradox is an essential element in her strategy, taking us beyond our customary use of concepts and images, forcing us to reinterpret them, to let them be transfigured and transformed. Yet as we should expect with Ann, the movement beyond, the moment of ecstasy, is lucid and sober. The precision remains. The union of the believer with God is eternal and inseparable, but it involves no confusion of mingling. It is a communion without intermediary, made possible in the full restoration of the image of God, that capacity for God which is latent in every person. It is a union which, at the supreme moment of her song, Ann can only express in terms of the kiss exchanged between the lover and the beloved, the bridegroom and the bride.

And here surely we must pause for a moment. In many ways it would be better to let these lines speak for themselves in all their simplicity, and to remain silent before them. But with their close juxtaposition of love and suffering depicted under such vivid imagery, they could be taken to suggest a kind of eroticism we do not usually find in Ann Griffiths' poetry. There are curious bypaths in the history of Christian devotion. What is the mystery of the wounds doing so close to the embrace of the beloved?

And here a second point has to be understood. Both images, the fellowship of the wounds, and the kiss of the beloved, carry with them a weight of hidden significance. Both phrases have scriptural overtones which give them a whole range of further associations. The words 'Kiss the Son' for instance occur in Psalm 2, v. 12 ('Kiss the son, lest he be angry, and so ye perish from the way') and are quoted by Ann in a quite different context. That the words as they occur in the hymn are full of personal longing, we need not deny. But they are something more than an expression of purely personal feeling. They form part of a sacred traditional text, which gives to them a certain objectivity and perspective, so that what is deeply personal does not become merely subjective, let alone sentimental. 'To kiss the Son', not lest he be angry, but so as never to turn from him any more, that is her desire, the desire which elsewhere she expresses in terms of her longing to be steadfast, to abide; to know the assurance of eternity and never to depart from it again.

Perhaps a parallel taken from a great Christian poem of our own century may help us to appreciate what Ann is saying here. *In Parenthesis* by David Jones is a very different kind of work from the hymns which we are considering. But it too contains much about wounds and death, because so much of it is about the experience of the ordinary foot-soldier in the trenches in Flanders in the First World War. It could be a profoundly depressing book, yet it is not. Throughout it there is a suggestion, implicit rather than explicit, that in and through the suffering and the sordidness, something of goodness is being revealed. As the author says in the preface, 'We find ourselves privates in foot regiments. We search how we may see formal goodness in a life singularly inimical, hateful to us'.

This suggestion that somehow what is evil is being redeemed by love becomes explicit only on the very last page of the book. There we are given six quotations from the Bible, three in the Latin of the Vulgate, three in the English of the Authorised Version. Thus it is made clear that while this is a very personal statement it is also a traditional one, gathering up the experience and the wisdom of many ages. Again it is done so as to distance us a little from the unbelievable poignancy of what is being said. For these quotations speak to us of the scapegoat which carries away the people's sins, of the lamb slain as a sacrificial victim, of the author of all form and comeliness without any form or comeliness; they speak to us of the suffering of Christ in the suffering of his people, and they conclude with the words from the Song of Songs, 'This is my beloved, and this is my friend'.

Yes, suffering and love are closely intermingled in human experience, and sometimes in perverse and destructive ways. The Christian tradition, when it is true to itself, is not afraid to enter into the dark and instinctual places of the human heart and mind. It would not have had very much power if it had not been willing to do so. But always it has believed that through the mystery of Christ the whole of humankind is brought back and redeemed. In Christ suffering itself be-

51

comes the way by which creative love is made free, and that creative and forigiving love is able to bring us to the eternal fulfillment for which, in the beginning, we were made.

FIVE

We have constantly to remember that the life which is reflected in the hymns was being lived in the day-to-day routine of a small farm in the Berwyns. There was a great deal to be done around the house and in the stockyard, and it would not always have been easy to reconcile the demands of the vision of ultimate and eternal realities with the requirements of every day.

We see something of the tension involved in Ann's letters. In one she writes,

> I am sometimes absorbed so far into these things that I completely fail to stand in the way of my duty with regard to temporal things. . . .

From the stories which have come down to us we can guess at some of the incidents she is referring to. Ann would be found in the kitchen, apparently unaware of all around her. A hymn was on the way. She would go out to the potato shed, but then not come back. After a time they would go and look for her and find her wholly lost in thought.

But there is much more to it than that. Reading Ann's letters we get the impression that there were periods of intense inner conflict. In the very first one she writes to John Hughes,

I should be glad to speak of my own experience. I have had some rather smart trials and strong winds, so that I was almost out of breath on the slopes . . .

And then, quoting two texts of Scripture which have helped her, she adds

I thought to pull myself up the hill by the two following chains . . . It was quiet and warm for a while.

This vivid way of speaking of inner trials in terms of daily experience on the hills continues in her later letters. But the sense of conflict grows stronger:

I have been finding it very stormy for a long time. I have had very many disappointments in myself without a break. . . . I have lately been particularly far gone in spiritual whoredom from the Lord.

Later she declares,

The warfare is as hot as it ever was, enemies within, enemies without.

What are we to make of such avowals?

First of all it is clear that Ann is living by very exalted standards. She seeks to abide in a vision of eternity while living in the midst of the changes of time. The overwhelming sense which she had of seeing into eternal things made demands on her whole life; it is difficult for us to enter into this fully. 'Of all things', she writes, 'it is the sin of thought which presses most heavily on me'. In another letter, she explains this more fully.

> The most pressing thing that is on my mind is the sinfulness of any visible thing obtaining a leading place in my mind. I am full of shame and reverence, and I rejoice in astonishment to think that he for whom it is a condescension to look upon the things of heaven has also given himself as an object of love to a creature as vile as I.

Here is the clue to understanding the sins and trials of which Ann speaks, her constant disappointment with herself. These things spring from her acute sense that if God can occupy the first place in her heart and mind, then it is a betrayal of his love, a denial of the very source of life and meaning, to allow anything else to take that first place. It is an infidelity, a refusal of his infinite generosity. Seen in this context, the language about spiritual harlotry, which of course is biblical in origin, does not seem so exaggerated. Clearly Ann allows that other things must enter in, must have their rightful place in her heart and mind. But even the best created things must never come before God; taken in comparison with him, who is by definition beyond all comparison, what are they but idols? And if this is the case with what is good, what about the hundred and one frivolous, trivial, unimportant thoughts and desires which flit through the mind in the course of a day? What about the malicious and destructive ones? It is in this perspective that we may hope to understand her 'longing to be pure', and her prayer to be steadfast and faithful to the vision. We remember that it is promised to the pure in heart that they shall see God, and we remember too, Kierkegaard's word, 'Purity of heart is to will one thing'.

As she went on along this perplexing path she grew in maturity. The letters cover a period of at most four years, and the dating of some of them is not altogether clear. But we can feel between the first and the last a definite growth in self-knowledge. She became more accustomed to the paradoxes involved in trying to live at different levels simultaneously, and discovered that alternations of light and darkness, times of stress and times of quiet, were an integral part of the way. Patience was needed, she found, as well as urgency. We must constantly be moving forward, but always be able to stand still and know by anticipation that completion which will be granted only in its fullness in the end of all things. She expresses this with a wonderful triple paradox in one hymn verse,

> I'll walk on softly day by day,
> The cross o'ershadowing all my way,
> And as I walk, my course I'll run
> And as I run I'll stand and see
> The full salvation that shall be
> When I'm no more beneath the sun.

As she followed on this way, however, she found that there were other possibilities of sinning against the light. Not only might she allow secondary things to come first in her thoughts and affections, but she might also allow her own ideas, her own imaginings, to take the place of the mysteries which God was revealing to her. To understand her anxieties here, we have to remember how seriously she would have taken the idea that the articles of Christian faith are not a matter of human invention, but God's own disclosure of himself. To fail to receive them lucidly and in due proportion is to dishonour him, and to risk cutting herself off from the very source of truth and light. If we wish to see how deeply Ann thought about this matter, to what a remarkable degree pure theology was important to her, we need to consider the following passage from the letter to Elizabeth Evans.

Dear sister, the most outstanding thing that is on my mind at present as a matter for thought is to do with grieving the Holy Spirit. That word came into my mind, 'Know ye not that your bodies are temples of the Holy Spirit which dwelleth in you'; and on penetrating a little into the wonders of the Person, and how he dwells or resides in the believer, I think in short that I have never been possessed to the same degree by reverential fears of grieving him, and along with that I have been able to see one reason, and the chief reason, why this great sin has made such a slight impression upon my mind, on account of my base and blasphemous thoughts about a Person so great.
This is how my thoughts ran about the Persons of the Trinity. I feel my mind being seized by shame, and yet under a constraint to speak because of the harmfulness of it. I thought of the persons of the Father and the Son

as co-equal; but as for the Person of the Holy Spirit, I regarded him as a functionary subordinate to them. O what a misguided imagination about a Person who is divine, all- present, all-knowing, and all-powerful to carry on and complete the good work which he has begun in accordance with the free covenant and the counsel of the Three in One regarding those who are the objects of the primal love. O for the privilege of being one of their number.

Dear sister, I feel a degree of thirst to grow up more in the belief in the personal indwelling of the Holy Spirit in my life; and this by way of revelation, not of imagination, as if I thought to comprehend in what way or by what means it happens, which is real idolatry.

This is not the place to discuss the profound theological intuition contained in this passage, the way in which Ann has expressed in a single sentence the tendency common to both main Christian traditions in the West to reduce the work of the Holy Spirit to a subsidiary element in the Christian scheme of things. But we should perhaps notice the explicit way in which she, whose imagination was evidently so strong, disclaims the use of her imagination, so sure is she that what she sees is not something of her own creation, which she could fully comprehend, but something which has been revealed to her, which she has been given. And we cannot help remarking on the depth of feeling revealed (*I feel my mind being seized by shame . . .*') over what many would consider a purely intellectual error of an abstract and remote kind.

For Ann everything which touches on Christian doctrine, and above all on the doctrines of the Trinity and the Incarnation, touches immediately the deepest things of her own life and experience, the way of salvation by which, she believes, a door is opened to her into a realm of everlasting truth and joy. Here as always, she speaks of God as if in the presence of God. She treats of the divine mysteries as of things into which she is already entering, into which she longs with all her being to enter further.

Indeed, the overwhelming impression which the letters convey is of one who is always pushing on, penetrating further into the apprehension of these things. It is the same movement that we find in the hymns. In one, she cries

O might I gain faith's insight,
With angel-minds on high,
Into Heaven's secret counsels,
Its saving mystery;
Two natures in one Person
Joined indivisibly,
True, pure and unconfounded,
Perfect in unity.

and in another,

O to pierce into the knowledge
Of the one, true, living Lord,
Slaying all imaginations,

59

Holding solely by the Word;
To believe what there stands written,
What from thence is clearly known: —
Sinners cannot live before him;
He, he only, must atone.

Like all the great Christian mystics, she seeks to penetrate
beyond all God's gifts to arrive at the Giver.

> I thought that we have to pass beyond brethren and
> graces, and love the Giver above the gifts. . . . It occurred
> to me that I should be content to give all that I possess,
> be it good or bad, to possess the Son, in a marriage
> union. . . . O to be at the feet of our good God as long
> as we are in the world.

God comes out from himself, from the unapproachable glory
of his transcendence, in order to enter creation and give himself to us, to make himself accessible to human knowledge
and human love. What can God's creatures do but respond
with a similar movement of ecstatic love, coming out from
themselves and their own small world of ideas and imaginations into the infinite greatness revealed in God's plan of
creation, in God's suffering love? Ann speaks of this in a
paragraph of one of her letters, where again we see very
clearly that the writer of the hymns and the writer of the letters are one and the same person: her power of handling images does not desert her when she takes to prose. Here, as in
other places, she is interpreting the Old Testament
throughout the prism of the New, so that the figure of King

60

Solomon immediately suggests to her the figure of the Christ, in whom all that Solomon stood for is summed up and fulfilled.

That word is on my mind tonight, 'Go forth, O ye daughters of Zion, and behold king Solomon with the crown wherewith his mother crowned him in the day of his espousals, and in the day of the gladness of his heart.' I think there is a high and peculiar calling for all who have part in the covenant to leave their own ceiled houses to see their King wearing the crown of thorns and the purple robe. No wonder the sun hid its rays when its Creator was pierced by nails. It is a marvel to me to think who it is that was on the cross, he whose eyes are as a flame of fire piercing through heaven and earth in a single glance, unable to see his creatures, the work of his hands. My mind is too overwhelmed to say anything more on the matter.

As we read on in her letters we find that the urgency of the desire to abide with God, to give all glory to God, increases:

I should heartily wish to give all the praise to God the Word, simply for leading me and upholding me so far, and that what remains of my life might be spent in continual communion with God in his Son, because I never can glorify him more than, or so much as by believing in and accepting his Son. Heaven help me do this, not

for my own pleasure alone, but out of reverence for
him.

Ann's whole thought and desire is centred upon God; it is his
glory, his praise, which always comes first. Human salvation
follows from it, but only as a consequence. It is this very fact
that makes her so grieved over the discovery of her own in-
constancy.

I am strongly bound to speak the praises of God, and
to be grateful to him for some degree of sharing in the
fellowship of the mystery. But here is my trouble —
failing to abide — continually departing. O for help to
abide.

Thomas Charles, after long conversation with Ann on
spiritual matters, is reputed to have told her that one of three
things would happen to her. She would die young, she
would suffer greatly, or else she would become a backslider.
Evidently he felt that such intensity of spiritual vision and
desire could hardly be maintained without some great cost.
'No one can see God and live'. When he mentioned the last
possibility to her, Ann wept. The first possibility was frequently in her mind. Seeing things so much in the light of
eternity, believing with such conviction that she was travelling towards that eternal realm, she inevitably thought much
about the transitoriness of earthly things, not least her own
life. Ann's last three letters are all signed with similar for-
mulas, 'This from your loving sister, swiftly journeying

through a world of time to the great world which lasts for ever'.

There is a feeling of haste about her, as of one for whom things are pressing. But her meditation on death, again a normal part of the traditional Christian way of life, does not take the form of a wish for death in itself. What she longs for is the steadfastness, the freedom from all that deflects her from God which, she believes, she will only find beyond that final frontier.

She herself puts the matter with her customary lucidity and balance:

Dear sister, I see more need than ever to spend my remaining days in giving myself up daily and continually, body and soul, into the care of him who is able to keep that which is committed unto him against that day. Not to give myself once, but to live continually giving myself, right up to and in the very moment when I put away this tabernacle. Dear sister, the thought of putting it away is particularly sweet sometimes. I can say that this is what cheers me more than anything else in these days, not death itself, but the great gain that is to be got through it. To be able to leave behind every inclination counter to the will of God, to leave behind every capacity to dishonour the law of God, all weakness swallowed up by strength, to become fully conformed to the law which is already on one's heart and to enjoy God's likeness for ever. Dear sister, I am sometimes absorbed so far into these things, that I completely fail to stand in the way of my duty with regard to temporal things, but I look for a time when I may find release and be with Christ, for that is very much better, although it is very good here through a lattice, and the Lord sometimes reveals through a glass, darkly, as much of his glory as my weak faculties can bear.

It is not surprising, in the light of such avowals as these, that some have been led to ask questions about Ann's marriage to Thomas Griffiths. How can it be that a woman who declares herself so wholly given to God can yet give herself to another in Christian marriage? Again, why is it, if she had to marry, that she did not marry John Hughes, with whom she evidently had so much in common? On the second and relatively minor question, I find the contention of Saunders Lewis generally convincing. Social distinctions were keenly felt in the countryside in eighteenth-century Wales; although, viewed from the outside, Ann's position seems modest enough, within her own world she was a person of some eminence. There was too great a social gap between the farmer's daughter and the weaver's apprentice for marriage to have been thinkable. John Hughes married Ruth Evans, Ann's maid and companion, and she was a witness at their wedding. Thomas Griffiths, whom Ann married, was not only a leading Methodist in the district but a farmer of some consequence as well.

As to the larger question of why Ann should have married at all, we may well reply with another: what else was she to do? Once her father was dead, it was evidently difficult for her to maintain the farm at Dolwar with only her brother's help. Every consideration of duty, social, domestic, and religious alike, would have suggested that marriage was the right course to take.

We need not disguise from ourselves the thought that had Ann lived in another time or another place, in Wales in the fourteenth century, or in France or Russia in the nineteenth, for instance, she would very possibly have found her place within a monastic community. The kind of contemplative nature which was hers could easily have found its fulfillment within the life of a community wholly given to the work of prayer and praise. Indeed, when her writing is introduced into such a milieu there is an immediate sense of kinship and recognition, as though she had come home. But in her own time such a possibility was in no way open to her. If such a way of life was known of at all in the circles in which she moved, it was known entirely at second hand, as a dangerous piece of superstitious and papistical error.

Marriage then would have presented itself to her as a duty. And why should it not also have presented itself as more? We have, it is true, no direct evidence one way or the other. We do not know exactly what were her feelings towards Thomas Griffiths of Meifod; but what little we know of him suggests that he was an eminently loveable man. Once we grant the overriding nature of the commitment to the love of God which is hers, we can surely allow the possibility that while no human love should displace it, a human love may well be compatible with it. On this subject we may hear an eminent and by no means radical Dominican scholar, Fr Festugière. He writes out of the heart of that Christian tradition which has most taken for granted the importance of a life of celibacy for anyone who wishes to give themself wholly to God. He is speaking here of George Herbert, but almost everything that he says could apply equally well to Ann.

As to knowing whether a *total* offering of oneself to God can be reconciled with a marriage for *love*, I leave it to God to judge. Certainly a sentence like 'he declared his resolution *both* to marry and to enter into the Sacred Order of Priesthood, has something surprising in it for the Catholic reader, at least down till today. But all ways are good and God is truly Lord and All. Herbert's friend, Nicholas Ferrar, refused an offer of marriage, asked to be ordained deacon and kept a voluntary celibacy; his two nieces, Mary and Anna Collett, made a private vow of virginity. Both Herbert and Ferrar left behind a reputation of holiness. And in any case, two facts are to be noted. (1) In the whole collection of The Temple, there is not a single poem relating to human love, (2) it is impossible to read this work without receiving the impression that Herbert was entirely given to God.

These latter points are in every way as true of Ann as of George Herbert. To suggest, as has been done, that her hymn- writing resulted from a disappointment in love, or that it ceased at the time of her marriage (both suppositions for which there is absolutely no evidence) argues a curious lack of sensitivity to the difference of quality between human and divine love. What is characteristic of Ann's writing, in hymns and letters alike, is that it reveals a love of strangely metaphysical character, a thirsting after eternity, a longing to be taken up into union with the source of life and all existence. It is a longing in which love and knowledge are fused together into one in a single movement of intense desire. There is something almost frightening in it. It is no wonder that, like Herbert and Ferrar before her, she should have left behind her a reputation for holiness, and that she should have been widely recognized as a 'saint', as nearly 'canonized' in that position as is possible in the Protestant tradition to which she belonged.

SIX

In view of the extreme narrowness of the external circumstances in which Ann's life was lived, it is one of the paradoxes of her work that her hymns and letters can convey such a sense of openness. Our way is open; we are not shut in or confined within a universe of space and time whose ultimate boundary is that of death. Indeed, it is this quality which is liable to make the reader feel a sense of personal indebtedness towards her, even if we are not able to see 'the plan of salvation' precisely as she sees it. Her writing communicates an extraordinarily powerful sense that human life can find its fulfillment, that all the ways are open before us into the kingdom of eternity.

There's an open door before me,
Means of victory in store,
Through the gifts he purchased for us
Who a servant's form once wore.

Through the power of Christ's triumph over death through death, Ann is able to say,

Principalities, dominations,
He their overthrow procured,

Spoiled them all, and jailed the jailer,
Through the passion he endured. . . .

When on high he reascended,
All his work fulfilled below,
Lofty gates their heads uplifted,
All their wondering joy to show;
Doors flew open, choirs sang welcome
To the Incarnate in that land,
And the Father, glad and radiant,
Bade him sit at his right hand.

Doors were opening. Through the substance of our daily life,
a way is opened into eternity. There can be for us no final
despair.

Ann's theme of the open door finds expression in other
hymns as the boldness and the freedom of access to God
which the believer possesses in Jesus Christ:

Boldly I will venture forward;
See the golden sceptre shine;
Pointing straight towards the sinner;
All may enter by that sign.
On I'll press, beseeching pardon,
On, till at his feet I fall,
Cry for pardon, cry for washing
In the Blood which cleanses all.

Here again Ann has identified herself in thought with one of
the great figures of the Old Testament, Esther, risking her life

on behalf of her people by venturing into the presence of King Ahasuerus, without being bidden. The king holds out his sceptre; all is well, she can go in.

This vision of the way in and the way forward finds its completest statement in the hymn which is totally given up to a meditation on Christ the Way. It is a hymn which, like all the others, is full of biblical allusions, but it is interesting too in that it seems to contain reference to the old Welsh proverb, 'let him that would be head, first be bridge', a proverb, it may be said, which has an extraordinary appositeness to the person of the Christ, as described in the New Testament.

Wholly counter to my nature
Is the path ordained for me;
Yet I'll tread it, yes, and calmly,
While thy precious face I see;
Count the cross a crown, and bear it,
Cheerful live 'mid all life's woes —
This the Way which, straight though tangled,
To the heavenly city goes.

Old it is, yet never aging,
And its name is Wonderful;
Ne'er begun, yet new for ever,
Making dead men rise up whole;
Winning all who travel by it;
Head and Husband 'tis to me;
Sacred way. I'll pass along it
Till in it my rest shall be.

This way into the land of promise is open to us, because already God's image is upon us and we are made in his likeness. It is this capacity for God that makes us more and more dissatisfied with the things of earth, taken in themselves, apart from him:

> Gladly would I leave behind me
> All the idols I have known,
> Since I bear inscribed the likeness
> Of a more exalted One;
> Worthy of unending worship,
> Love, and reverence is he;
> By his precious death were myriads
> From the jaws of death set free.

Indeed this thought of the growing likeness between creature and Creator emboldens Ann to pray in one hymn that her soul may be adorned with the divine likeness.

> Let me, clothed in thine own likeness,
> In thy hand a terror be,
> Hell, ungodliness, corruption
> Tremble at the sight of me.
> Seal me with thy name, whose fragrance
> Is diffused in every place,
> Salting all the world, and sweetening
> With the beauteous gifts of grace.

She is being clothed with the attributes of God; she is becoming already, by means of God's gift, that which God is by nature.

But of course in this life we are only setting out on this way. Here the likeness is only revealed in part. So in another hymn she prays,

> Let me drink for ever deeply
> Of salvation's mighty flood,
> Till I thirst no more for ever
> After any earthly good;
> Live expectant of his coming,
> Watchful every hour abide,
> Haste to open, and be fully
> With his likeness satisfied.

If we find in these verses an insistence on the passing nature of this world, an emphasis on the necessity of leaving aside all created things, which disturbs us, still we must surely recognize that this movement away from the earth is far from being purely negative. It is not renunciation for the sake of renunciation, but rather that Ann has seen something else, something which she strains all her powers to convey to us, and exhorts us to turn aside from finite things which can never wholly satisfy our hearts and minds.

> I shall feel a mighty wonder
> When that blessed hour finds birth
> When my mind, that here goes wandering
> After the mean toys of earth.
> Finds its undistraught devotion

To his Person henceforth given,
And unshakably conforming
To the holy laws of heaven.

In another hymn she writes,

Sweet to think upon the cov'nant
Made on high ere time began,
Gazing ever on the Person
Who assumed the form of man;
Unto death his soul was troubled,
All the agreement to fulfil;
Now the ransomed seven-score-thousand
Shout and sing on Zion's hill.

There no fiery sun at noonday
Smites; there death itself is slain;
Freed from sorrow, there the blessed
Sing of One in mortal pain;
There they swim in life's pure river
Flowing from the holy Three,
'Neath those peaceful rays unclouded
Streaming down from Calvary.

There is in any life that has been marked by a peculiar
genius the capacity to sum up and express the life of a great
multitude of people. A politician who speaks for the nation
in its time of need may do it in one way, a great artist in
another. But in a life whose significance and intention is ex-
plicitly religious, this can happen in a particularly universal

way. For here there is a wrestling with the ultimate questions of human life. Is there a way along which we may go? Is it a way that leads to any goal, or is it doomed to end in futility? Here the final questions of meaning and meaninglessness are constantly and directly confronted.

In the case of Ann Griffiths, we have a woman in whose life the things of many ages and of many peoples come together into one. The great abiding images of the Bible come to new life. The central affirmations of Christian faith — that God puts on human flesh so that we may enter into that communion of life and love which is in God — find new and powerful expression. As has already been said, she stands at the centre of the Christian tradition of prayer and faith; despite the limitations of her writings, her stature is to be measured against the great and unquestioned figures of the Church's history, such as Teresa of Avila, Julian of Norwich, or Hildegaard of Bingen. But this place which is hers within the universal chorus of the Church's praise, in no way cuts her off from her own people, from the nation which gave her birth. For it is the characteristic of holiness, the life of God, that when it touches the things of earth it destroys separations without destroying distinctions. It creates harmony and peace without eliminating diversity and richness. So it is that Ann stands within the long tradition of prayer and of the praise of God which first burst out in Wales in the age of saints, which ran as a kind of bass line under the exuberant counterpoint of the poetry of the middle ages, to break out again in the apparently unpropitious circumstances of the late eighteenth century. Here in the Berwyns at a moment when in Europe the meaning of this tradition was largely being forgotten, a life was lived in the light of eternity, 'swiftly travelling through the world of time to the great world which lasts for ever'. It was a life in which the things of earth were constantly mingled with the things of heaven, in which the joy which can light up human life below, was constantly associated with the rejoicing of the angelic powers. It was in itself a point of intersection of the timeless with time, a place where the narrowness of this world opens out onto the spaces of the great world which lasts for ever. As R. S. Thomas puts it in his poem 'Fugue for Ann Griffiths'

Here for a few years
the spirit sang on a bone bough
at eternity's window, the flesh trembling
at the splendour of a forgiveness
too impossible to believe in, yet believing.

There is much here which we may feel that we do not understand, much that eludes our comprehension or our belief. But what we do see, whether it be little or whether it be much, is something that gives grounds for hope, grounds for faith, grounds for love, in a world which knows itself to be desperately in need of these things.

PART TWO

LETTERS AND HYMNS

To John Hughes
Dear Brother,   December 28, 1800

I have had this opportunity to send you these few lines in order to show my readiness to receive and answer your substantial letter, as I fully believe that it was in the field of Boaz that you gleaned the ears of corn, so full and so charged with blessing, which you have sent me, bidding me rub them and feed on them, and I think they will take so much effect on my mind as to make me sigh for the Rock. For you could not have sent any thing more pertinent to my condition, as was your intention because you knew more of my story in all its troubles than anyone else. I am glad, glad, to hear of your perseverance in meditation on your condition and in the Word, and I wish you prosperity in everything.

As for us at Pont, in bodily health as usual, and on the spiritual side the Association as a whole body is more alert, and the ministry generally full of unction. I have not much to say at present about particular persons, but I should be glad to speak of my own experience. I have had some very smart trials, and strong winds, so that I was almost out of breath on the slopes, but I thought to pull myself up the hill by the following two chains, 'And a Man shall be as an hiding place' etc., and 'Come, my people, —and hide thyself' etc. It was quiet and warm for a time.

I have had another trial concerning the time I have lived in the Church of God, having made my religious decision on wrong grounds from the start, and thinking of giving up. I was lifted up thus, 'seeing that we have a great High Priest' etc. But at present very cloudy and doubtful about myself, with the question beating upon my mind whether a true work has been begun in me or not. But in face of everything, I say 'though he slay me', etc.

We have had very precious privileges in these past days, the Ordinance twice, and a sweet savour at the breaking of the bread.

Dear brother, I was glad to hear your point about the circumstances of God's church being made clear to professed believers, because I think I am not altogether a stranger to this in these troublous days of the winnowing of Zion. All awakened Christians are specially bound in this matter to grieve over the sight of the stones of the sanctuary lying at the end of every street, through impurity, theft, and the like. I desire of you to take the Bride of the Lamb to the throne of grace. Pray with much sighing for her restoration. Draw her to her Bridegroom, because 'God hath not cast away his people which he foreknew', because the covenant is a covenant by oath, however corrupt she may be. Two scriptures in particular have been on my mind, one mentioned above, and the other is this, 'the cup is in the hand of the Lord, and the wine is red; it is full mixed, and it is poured out of the same; and all the ungodly of the earth shall drink the lees thereof'. Light has dawned on my mind. For if one of the cups that are spoken of is poured out the children will only be purged, because they are in a Father's hand. But let us pray for help to suffer the discipline, be it bitter as it may, so that we may attain our place.

Well, I will stop here. From your fellow-pilgrim on the journey to eternity.

Ann Thomas, Dolwar

To John Hughes
Dear Brother in the Lord,   February 17, 1801

I take the opportunity to send you these lines to let you know that I have received your letters with pleasure, hoping that the weighty things contained in them will find lodging in my mind.

I am glad to hear of your experience in relation to your condition. Precious is a friend who sticks close, as you say.

A thought has struck me which it would perhaps be worth while for me to mention, on the passage 'Simon, son of Jonas, lovest thou me more than these?' I thought that we have to pass beyond brethren and graces, and love the Giver above the gift.

Another word has taken hold of my mind, 'Buy the truth and sell it not'. It occurred to me that I should be content to give all that I possess, be it good or evil, to possess the Son, in a marriage union. It is in my mind that every careless word, and all levity of spirit, and all behaviour which appears contrary to Gospel holiness, is a total denial that we have known Jesus Christ. But in face of our great wretchedness, how precious it is to think of this word, 'the Lord turned and looked upon Peter'.

I am cheered by the thought that a sinner is free to speak so much of Jesus Christ before the throne of grace, while heaven smiles and hell trembles. Let us magnify our privilege in having come to know something of the effects of the eternal covenant decreed above. O to remain under the dew of the sanctuary until the evening, and to recognize that it has been purchased by blood. That would bring sinners down to the dust. O to be at the feet of our good God as long as we are in the world. Well, I will send you some account of the experience of the Association at Pont. In general richly bedewed, and wide awake as regards the greater part of the Church at present. I think we are no strangers to the wine which is distributed among the disciples here on their journey.

If I come to speak of my own experience, I should wish to bless God for remembering me in face of many doubts. I have never seen so much reason to cry out for the Rock in all weathers. And whether I die or live, this is my cry, O to be 'in him, with nothing of my own righteousness, which is of the law'. I have heard a parable of a shopkeeper who went to Chester to buy two hundred pounds' worth of goods, and made an inventory and hung it up in the shop, naming and detailing his possessions, and a man came in and asked for a crown's worth of one of them. He replied that he had not a pennyworth of it. Though many may make a grand show in the profession of religion, yet in face of temptation you ask, Where is their faith? A cry has arisen, little children, shout, for the wagon has come home, it is heavily loaded; viz. the ministers of the Word.

Well, I will stop. This from one who longs to desire the prosperity of those who journey to Zion.

Ann Thomas, Dolwar

To John Hughes,
Dear Brother,   undated
   I have had this opportunity to write to you, hoping you
are well, and to let you know I have received your precious
letter. I hope you will not neglect to send what is profitable,
and not pay attention to our own neglectfulness, because you
know the cause of it, our lack of anything of value to send.
   Dear brother, I should be glad to see you many times when
I am in distress of mind and gnawed by doubts of the
genuineness of the visitations, and the partial revelations of
a Mediator, in view of my damnable and lost condition. And
in spite of trying many roads, failing to achieve my purpose.
But I have sometimes found a road of meditation from the
passage where Moses' father- in-law advises him to set up
sixty leaders to judge the people in cases which are commonplace and easily seen through, but to bring great and
obscure cases to him. I have thought that in my perplexing
situation it is necessary to pass beyond the watchers of the
city and everything else, to God alone. It is a comfort to me
to think of this, that when my condition is most dark to me
and my brethren, it is clear as daylight in the court of the High
Priest. Thanks always for this.
   I have found much pleasure in meditating on the Shunammite woman who set aside a room on the wall for the man of
God to rest in when he passed by, placing in it a bed, a table,
a stool and a candlestick. Perhaps this woman, in her longing for the prophet, often paced the room, and found a satisfaction in watching for the the man. But however that may
be, it comforts the heart of a believer, in the absence of the
visible countenance of her Lord, that in some sense the fur-

niture is still there. For one thing, it is a sign that she has not given him up. For another thing, the lodging is too hot for a devil. When the enemy comes in like a strong river, the spirit of the Lord chases him out. He cannot so much as raise his hand in the temple of God without trembling, or look upon anything within it, except the track of his own feet, without fear. Therefore let us often entreat that the Holy Spirit may make his home in us.

Dear brother, things are somewhat dark at present for the Church at pont, under fire from the world and from back-sliders. I found great pleasure one evening in view of all these things in thinking what the Holy Spirit says to us. Two scriptures were on my mind, 'Glorious things are spoken of thee, O city of God'. 'The Lord thy God in the midst of thee is mighty'.

That is all at present from your sister.

Ann Thomas, Dolwar

To John Hughes
Dear Brother, undated
It has many times been a great pleasure to me to send you my experience. I have received much pleasure and blessing from reading your letters, which moves me very strongly to beg you earnestly not to hold your hand.

Dear brother, the warfare is as hot now as it ever was, enemies within, enemies without. But of all things, it is the sin of thought which presses most heavily upon me. I find particular pleasure today in thinking of this word, 'And to Jesus, the mediator of the New Testament, and the blood of sprinkling'. Something new here in the way of love for the doctrine of purification. This word is on my mind, 'And the blood of Jesus Christ his Son cleanseth us from all sin'. I have never had a greater longing to be pure. This word is on my mind, 'The house, when it was in building, was built of stones that had been fully dressed'. I sometimes think I have no desire ever to change my garment, but a longing to be pure in my garment. I should be well pleased to remain more in the sanctuary, as you explain so fully and usefully. I often expect to encounter troublesome weather, though I do not know just what. This word is on my mind tonight, 'By this shall the iniquity of Jacob be purged', etc. O for help to abide with God, whatever comes my way. And thanks always that the furnace and the fountain are so close together.

There is nothing else in particular on my mind at present, but please remember me often, and send to me soon. I, your unworthy sister, love your prosperity in body and spirit.

Ann Thomas, Dolwar

To John Hughes

Dear Brother in the Lord,   undated

I am writing to you now because it is the natural rum of my thoughts, in face of all kinds of weather, to tell my story to you, dear brother.

Dear brother, the most outstanding thing that is on my mind is the great obligation I am under to be grateful to the Lord for upholding me in face of the winds and the flood waters. I may say that my thoughts have never been brought to the same pitch of fear as in these days; but in face of everything I think to hang quietly upon this precious promise, 'When thou passest through the waters, I will be with thee'. I think it is enough to support me in the place where two seas meet. Thanks always for a God who fulfills his promises.

Dear brother, the most pressing thing that is on my mind is the sinfulness of letting any visible thing obtain a leading place in my thoughts. I am full of shame and reverence, rejoicing and marvelling at the thought that he for whom it is a condescension to look upon the things in heaven has also given himself as an object of love to a creature as vile as I.

As regards the dishonour done to God by giving the first place to secondary things, here in simple terms is what I think. If nature must needs be pressed into the grasp of death because it is too weak to bear the fiery rays of the sun of temptations, I sometimes think I can see myself gladly stripped of my natural life (if need be) rather than that glory should go under a cloud while nature gets its own way and its objects.

This word is on my mind tonight, 'Go forth, O ye daughters of Zion, and behold King Solomon with the crown wherewith his mother crowned him in the day of his espousals, and in the day of the gladness of his heart'. I think there is a high and peculiar calling for all who are partakers in the covenant to leave their own ceiled houses to see their King wearing the crown of thorns and the purple robe. No wonder the sun hid its rays when its Creator was pierced by nails. It is a marvel to me to think who it was that was on the cross, he whose eyes are as a flame of fire piercing through heaven and earth at once, unable to see his creatures, the work of his hands. My mind is too overwhelmed for me to say anything more on the matter. But if we look at the greatness of the person, it is no wonder that his word has been set down. 'The Lord will be well pleased for his righteousness' sake, he will magnify the law and make it honorable'. Dear brother, it is no wonder that this word has been set down, 'Kiss the Son lest he be angry'.

Dear brother, there is nothing special on my mind in addition to this at present. But this I will say deliberately, I desire that the remaining part of my life should be in communion so close that it might never again belong to me to say, 'I will go and I will return'. I should think, if only this could be, I should be calm to meet Providence with its frowns and its crosses. I desire a special place in your prayers. Remember to send soon. I am longing for a letter.

I am
Your loving sister
Ann Thomas, Dolwar

To John Hughes
Dear Brother and Father in the Lord,   April, 1802
I received your letter yesterday, and it was a great pleasure to me to have it. I hope the precious things which are in it will be a blessing to me. I was very pleased with the Scripture which you remarked upon in my brother's letter.

But to proceed to tell you something of my present experience. I have been finding it very stormy for a long time now. Very many disappointments in myself, without a break. But this I must say, that all trials, all winds, of whatever sort, work together to one end, namely, to bring me to see more of my wretched condition by nature, and more of the Lord in his goodness and unchangeableness towards me. I have lately been particularly far gone in spiritual whoredom from the Lord, while yet holding up my head in face of the ministry like one staying dutifully at home and remaining in the fellowship. But in spite of all my skill the Lord of his goodness uttered these words, 'If I be a father, where is mine honour? If I be a master, where is my fear?' Thanks to God always for the bolts of heaven which come flying where there is sickness. My stomach was so weak that I could not feed on God's free mercy, in view of the path I was following, having forsaken God, the fountain of all real consolations, and hewn out for myself broken cisterns. This word did something to put me on my feet again, 'The Lord is my shepherd, I shall not want'. I going astray, he a shepherd; I powerless to return, he an almighty Lord. O rock of our salvation, wholly self-dependent in the matter of saving sinners. Dear brother, I should wish to be for ever under the discipline, be it as bitter as it may.

Another word was a special blessing to me lately when I tried to speak to the Lord about the various things which were calling me to go after them. This is the word, 'Look unto me, all the end of the earth, that ye may be saved, for I am God, and not another'. As if God were saying, 'I know about all the things that call to you, and how various they are, but I myself am calling. The world is only the world, the flesh is only the flesh, and the devil is only the devil, it is I who am God, and no one else'.

I am constrained to be grateful for the Word in its invincible authority. I should heartily wish to give all the praise to God the Word, simply for leading me and upholding me so far, and that what remains of my life should be spent in abiding communion with God in his Son, because I can never glorify him more than, or so much as, by believing in and accepting his Son. Heaven help me to do this, not for my own pleasure alone, but out of reverence for him.

Dear brother, there is not much else on my mind to add to this, but think often of Zion throughout the world, and in particular of your Mother at Pont, for the shades of evening are on the point of covering her, and grey hairs are here and there upon her, and in a small measure she knows this. This word is much on my mind, and on other people's minds too, at the sight of the weak, aimless, dejected appearance she presents, 'Is this Naomi?' Wrestle much with the Lord in prayer for her sake, as a body of witnesses for God in the world, because his great name is in some measure being obscured by her in our backslidings.

Dear brother, I am very pleased to hear your story in connection with your new work. Two scriptures have been on my mind with reference to it, one — 'Thus shall it be done unto the man whom the king delighteth to honor'; and the other, 'Surely the Lord's anointed is before me, but God sees not as man sees, that is why they had to send for David'.

Well, I will close now, with a request to you to send to me speedily. I am your unworthy sister, running swiftly towards the world that lasts for ever.

Ann Thomas, Dolwar

To John Hughes
Dear Brother,   undated
I take the opportunity to send to you these few lines to let you know that I received your letter with pleasure, and am glad to have an opportunity to send you my present experience.

Dear brother, I have never talked with you or written to you with such a low view of myself as this time; and I am ashamed to think that I ever had a different view. This word has come into my mind — 'I have set before thee an open door, and no man can shut it, for thou hast a little strength'. Thanks for ever to the God of all grace for taking his precious Word in his hand to discipline me; I reverently believe that so it is, and that his weapons and his blows are continually at the root of selfishness which is so strong in my corrupt nature. I have received more light on my lost condition in the last few days than in the whole time of my profession, and more on the glory of God's wise design in justifying the ungodly, and that he was in Christ reconciling the world to himself, not imputing their trespasses unto them. I am often at the throne of grace in wonder and thanksgiving and prayer; wondering that the Word and the Holy Spirit should have found a way to handle the condition of such a corrupt wretch, full of guile, without killing me. Thanks for the lawfulness of the way of salvation; and that because it glorifies its author, more than because it rewards those who travel along it. I pray that I may spend the remnant that is left of my days in a life of fellowship with God in his Son Jesus Christ, the great Mediator between God and men. It would be a very precious thing to me if I could be saved from venturing to offer to God's holy law more than that which has satisfied it; not because it does not admit of anything else, but out of reverence for it. I never before knew so much reverence towards and love for the law; not in spite of the fact that it brings a curse, but just because it brings a curse everywhere where there is not a Mediator; because thus it shows its beauty and its perfection.

Dear brother, I was glad to read the letter you sent to my brother, and also your letter to S.G. and your exhortations to read and search the Scriptures; I am thinking what our state could possibly be if we had not the Word, and according to the Word itself it would be this, that we should be spending money for that which is not bread, and our labour for that which satisfieth not; because the stomach of the new nature does not agree with anything else; and all winds bring sickness except those which blow from the sanctuary. The following words have been of great value and comfort to my soul of late —'Thy neck is like the tower of David builded for an armoury; whereon there hang a thousand bucklers, all shields of mighty men'. In myself I am powerless and without arms to face enemies, but if I receive the privilege of turning to the tower, I shall find there arms and strength to run through the troop. These words too have been of great comfort to me — 'It pleased the Father that in him should all fullness dwell'; and also these words — 'A garden enclosed is my sister, my bride I am strongly bound to speak the praises of God, and to be grateful to him for some degrees of sharing in the fellowship of the mystery'. But here is my trouble — failing to abide — continually departing. O for help to abide. This word is much in my mind — 'Meditate upon these things, and in these things abide'. I desire you to send me your view on this word —' In all points tempted like as we are, yet without sin'. The depressed appearance presented by God's cause in some places in these days weighs seriously upon my mind. All awakened souls are strongly bound to wrestle much with God in earnest prayer that he may send the winds to breathe upon his drooping garden, that its spices may be spread abroad; that Satan and all who have part in his kingdom may be unable to breathe through the strength of the perfume.

Now to conclude. I desire you to remember me at the throne of grace. I desire you to send me a letter at the first opportunity. This from your unworthy sister, swiftly travelling through the world of time to the world which lasts forever.

Ann Thomas, Dolwar

To Elizabeth Evans
My dear Sister in the Lord, undated
In accordance with your wish I write these few lines to you, and I am very glad to have an opportunity to make my experience known to you. Dear sister, the most outstanding thing that is on my mind at present as a matter for thought has to do with grieving the Holy Spirit. This word came into my mind, 'Know ye not that your bodies are temples of the Holy Ghost which dwelleth in you?' And on penetrating a little into the wonders of the Person, and how he dwells or resides in the believer, I think in short that I have never been possessed to the same degree by reverential fears of grieving him, and along with this I have been unable to see one reason, and the chief reason, why this great sin has made such a slight impression and weighed so lightly upon my mind, on account of my base and blasphemous thoughts about a Person so great.

This is how my thoughts ran about the Persons of the Trinity. I hear my mind being seized by shame, and even inhibited from speaking on account of the harmfulness of this. I thought of the Persons of the Father and the Son as coequal; but as for the Person of the Holy Spirit, I regarded him as a functionary subordinate to them. O what a misguided imagination about a Person who is divine, all-present, all-knowing, and all-powerful to carry on and complete the good work which he has begun in accordance with the covenant of grace and the counsel of the Three in One regarding those who are the objects of the primal love. O for the privilege of being one of their number.

Dear sister, I feel a degree of thirst to grow up more in the belief in the personal indwelling of the Holy Spirit in my life; and this by way of revelation, not of my own imagination, as if I thought to comprehend in what way or by what means it happens, which is real idolatry.

Dear sister, when I look a little at the inherent sinfulness of grieving the Holy Spirit, and on the other hand look into the depths of the great Fall and see myself wholly divested of all power to do anything but grieve him, I am indeed somewhat in a strait. But this word is on my mind, 'Watch and pray'; as if the Lord were saying,'Although the commandment is so stiff, and thou art so powerless to fulfill one thing in a thousand in yonder place on yonder earth because of the condition of thy mind, come forth, make trial of the throne, for the fervent prayer of the righteous availeth much; my grace is sufficient for thee, my strength is made perfect in weakness'. Thanks always for a God who fulfills his promises.

Dear sister, I should like to say much about the virtue of secret prayer, but you know more than I can say about it, but I am fully convinced that it is much the best thing for meeting enemies and the host of armed men. I know from experience, through finding myself surrounded by enemies, that I could find nothing to say but this — 'And I give myself to prayer'. . . . O for the privilege of being under the detailed supervision of the Holy Ghost, I think quite simply that my condition will never be met by a supervision less detailed than is expressed in this word, 'I will water it every moment'. Thanks always for a Bible which fits a condition that has sunk so deep. Dear sister, it is a great privilege that one's condition can be found reflected in God's Word. O to hold it up to the holy mirror to the end that we may make use of a mediator.

One thing in particular on my mind last night with regard to finding one's condition in the Word. R.J. said some very valuable things on the subject, and there was I so dry, so out of touch as regards my experience, neither Law nor Gospel had any effect on me, and this brought a degree of fear into my mind, failing to think I could find my condition in the word because Law and Gospel were seemingly useless. This word came into my mind, 'Go thy way forth by the footsteps of the flock'; and I could not see the footsteps of the flock in this situation. But this word came into my mind with light and warmth, 'Awake, O north wind, and come, thou south'. Thanks always for the rock of the Word to set foot on as a start, and the impossibility of starting without it.

Dear sister, I see more need than ever to spend my remaining days in giving myself up daily and continually, body and soul, into the care of him who is able to keep that which is committed unto him against that day. Not to give myself once, but to live continually giving myself, right up to and in the very moment when I put away this tabernacle. Dear sister, the thought of putting it away is particularly sweet sometimes, I can say that this is what cheers me more than anything else in these days, not death in itself, but the great gain that is to be got through it. To be able to leave behind every inclination that goes against the will of God, to leave behind every ability to dishonour the law of God, with all weakness swallowed up by strength, to become fully conformed to the law which is already on one's heart and to enjoy God's likeness forever. Dear sister, I am sometimes absorbed so far into these things that I completely fail to stand in the way of my duty with regard to temporal things, but I look for the time when I may find release and be with Christ, for it is very much better, although it is very good here through a lattice, and the Lord sometimes reveals through a glass, darkly, as much of his glory as my weak faculties can bear.

Dear sister, I am glad to say this deliberately, I should like to say it with thankfulness, in spite of all my corruption, and the devices of hell, the world and its objects, through God's goodness alone I have not changed the object of my love until tonight; but rather I desire from my heart to find contentment in his love and to be glad in him perpetually with singing, although I cannot attain to this in the slightest degree on this side of death except by violence.

My dear sister, I particularly desire you to send to me with speed; do not refuse me, I shall not be able to help taking it unkindly if you do. Ruth wishes to be remembered kindly to you. I have nothing in particular to send to you by way of news except this, that there is a spirit abroad of hoping everything to find signs of the recovery of Rachel Pugh. This from your loving sister, swiftly journeying through a world of time to the great world which lasts forever.

Ann Thomas

Wholly counter to my nature
Is the path ordained for me;

Yet I'll tread it, yes, and calmly,
While thy precious face I see;
Count the cross a crown, and bear it,
Cheerful life 'mid all life's woes —
This the Way which, straight though tangled,
To the heavenly city goes.

1.

The bells are sweetly ringing
Great Jesus' robes around;
The odour of pomegranates
Suffuses all the ground;
Forgiveness for the sinner,
And peace and joy supplied
Through him whose faultless offering
The Father satisfied.

2.

Follow on behind the reapers,
'Mid the sheaves thy dwelling make;
When mount Sinai burns and trembles,
At the cross thy morsel take;
See thy God, in his deep counsels,
At thy feet an altar raise;
God-in-man is suffering on it;
Cry for light to sing his praise.

3.

There's an opening door before me,
Means of victory in store,
Through the gifts he purchased for us
Who a servant's form once wore.
Principalities, dominations,
He their overthrow procured,
Spoiled them all, and jailed the jailer,
Through the passion he endured.

When I think upon that battle,
My sad soul leaps up with glee;
See! the law is held in honour,
Yet transgressors walk forth free;
See! our Resurrection's buried,
And our Life laid underground;
See! our earth with highest heaven
In eternal peace is bound.

When on high he reascended,
All his work fulfilled below,
Lofty gates their heads uplifted,
All their wondering joy to show;
Doors flew open, choirs sang welcome
To the Incarnate in that land,
And the Father, glad and radiant,
Bade him sit at his right hand.

'Tis enough 'mid flooding waters,
'Tis enough 'mid flames of fire;
Cling to him, my soul, for ever,
Follow him, and never tire;
On Arabia's desert pathways
Foes unnumbered wait for me;
Grant a share in his dear passion
Who was slain on Calvary.

4.

Here within the tent of meeting
Is the blood that can atone,
Here the slayer's place of refuge,
Here a healer's power made known;
Here a place, hard by the Godhead,
For the sinner's nest to lie,
While the righteousness of heaven
Smiles on him perpetually.

Sinner is my name and nature,
Fouler none on earth can be;
In the Presence here — O wonder! —
God receives me tranquilly;
See him there, his law fulfilling,
For his foes a banquet laid,
God and man "Enough!" proclaiming
Through the offering he has made.

Boldly I will venture forward;
See the golden sceptre shine;
Pointing straight towards the sinner;
All may enter by that sign.
On I'll press, beseeching pardon,
On, till at his feet I fall,
Cry for pardon, cry for washing
In the blood which cleanses all.

O to come, like smoky pillars,
From the desert to the throne
Where with countenance unclouded
Sits our royal Solomon.
Faithful Witness, never changing,
God's Amen ere time began,
He displays the Triune glory
In his saving work for man.

5.

Pilgrim, faint and tempest-beaten,
Lift thy gaze, behold and know
Christ the Lamb, our Mediator,
Robed in vestments trailing low;
Faithfulness his golden girdle;
Bells upon his garments ring
Free salvation for the sinner
Through his priceless offering.

Think on this when to your ankles
Scarce the healing waters rise —
Numberless shall be the cubits
Measured to you in the skies.
Children of the resurrection,
They alone can venture here;
Yet they find no shore, no bottom
To Bethesda's waters clear.

O the deeps of our salvation!
Mystery of godliness!
He, the God of gods, appearing
In our fleshly human dress;
He it is who bore God's anger,
In our place atonement made,
Until Justice cried 'Release him,
Now the debt is fully paid'.

Blessed hour of rest eternal,
Home at last, all labours o'er;
Sea of wonders never sounded,
Sea where none can find a shore;
Access free to dwell for ever
Yonder with the One in Three;
Deeps no foot of man can traverse —
God and Man in unity.

6.

Wholly counter to my nature
Is the path ordained for me;
Yet I'll tread it, yes, and calmly,
While thy precious face I see;
Count the cross a crown, and bear it,
Cheerful live 'mid all life's woes —
This the Way which, straight though tangled,
To the heavenly city goes.

Old it is, yet never aging,
And its name is Wonderful;
Ne'er begun, yet new for ever,
Making dead men rise up whole;
Winning all who travel by it;
Head and Husband 'tis to me;
Sacred way, I'll pass along it
Till in it my rest shall be.

Eye of kite could ne'er discern it,
Though it shines with noontide blaze;
None can tread it, none can see it,
Save where faith its light displays;
Breaking ne'er the law of justice,
Godless souls it justifies,
Leads them to God's peace and favor,
Bids the dead to life arise.

Way made straight before creation,
Kept to be revealed at need,
When in days of old, in Eden,
God proclaimed the woman's Seed;
His new covenant's foundation,
Once decreed ere time began,
'Tis the wine whose ample virtue
Glads the heart of God and man.

7.

Now the royal seed are summoned
To their land beyond the sea,
Freed from bondage in the brickworks,
There to reign eternally.
Yonder, faith is turned to vision,
Hope enjoys its promised good;
There they all, in endless anthem,
Glorify the precious blood.

Gladly would I leave behind me
All the idols I have known,
Since I bear inscribed the likeness
Of a more exalted One;
Worthy of unending worship,
Love, and reverence is he;
By his precious death were myriads
From the jaws of death set free.

Sweetly spreads my spikenard's fragrance
While I feast on love unbought,
Flame with zeal against all evil,
Cherish every holy thought;
Eye and right hand flinging from me,
Lofty looks to earth bring down;
Jesus over all exalting,
Him alone with worship crown.

Let me only live to hallow
God's pure name till life shall end,
Bow before his will, and welcome
All his providence may send,
Vow, and pay my vows, receiving
From the Lord's rich treasure-store
Grace to strengthen and to crown me
Victor in the conflict sore.

Let me, clothed in thine own likeness,
In thy hand a terror be,
Hell, ungodliness, corruption
Tremble at the sight of me.
Send me with thy name, whose fragrance
Is diffused in every place,
Salting all the world, and sweetening
With the beauteous gifts of grace.

8.

O might I gain faith's insight,
With angel-minds on high,
Into Heaven's secret counsels,
Its saving mystery;
Two natures in one Person
Joined indivisibly,
True, pure and unconfounded,
Perfect in unity.

Behold him all-sufficient,
My soul, thy need to fill;
Take heart, and cast upon him
The weight of every ill;
True man, in all thy weakness
He truly feels for thee;
True God, o'er world, flesh, Satan
He reigns victoriously.

Each day from the fierce conflict
I long to turn aside —
Not leave the ark, or Israel,
But turn from human pride,
And come to the King's table,
Who bids me go up higher,
When in the dust to love him
Was all I durst desire.

Though strong may be the tempests
And swellings of the sea,
Yet Wisdom is the pilot;
A mighty Lord is he;
Though sin comes flooding round me,
Its billows rising fast,
The ark is God almighty,
And all is safe at last.

9.

Even when the soul most ardent
Burns the most with living fire,
It can ne'er to the perfection
Of God's holy law aspire;
O that I might pay it honour
By accepting his free grace,
And in that most sweet communion,
Through the blood, might find a place.

I shall feel a mighty wonder
When that blessed hour finds birth
When my mind, that here goes wandering
After the mean toys of the earth,
Finds its undistraught devotion
To his Person henceforth given,
And unshakably conforming
To the holy laws of heaven.

10.
  Wonderful to come out living
  From the fiery furnace-blast,
  But yet more, that after testing
  I shall be fine gold at last;
Time of cleansing! Time of winnowing!
  Yet 'tis calm, without dismay;
  He who soon shall be my refuge
  Holds the winnowing-fan today.

  Weary is my life, by foemen
  Thick beset in savage throng,
  For like bees they come about me,
  Harass me the whole day long;
  They of mine own house and kindred
  Captain the infernal brood;
But, through grace the strife sustaining,
  I'll contend even unto blood.

11.

Since I'm so corrupt by nature,
Straying from thee constantly,
'Tis for me a grace transcendent
On thy holy mount to be;
Here the veils are rent asunder,
All concealment done away;
Thou thine all-excelling glory
Over all things dost display.

Let me drink for ever deeply
Of salvation's mighty flood,
Till I thirst no more for ever
After any earthly good;
Live expectant of his coming,
Watchful every hour abide,
Haste to open, and be fully
With his likeness satisfied.

12.

O that all my head were waters,
Weeping ever, day and night,
Since the bannered hosts of Zion
Flinch and falter in the fight.
O reveal the shining pillars
Given of old her strength to be,
Promises divine, unchanging,
Won for us on Calvary.

Lord, thy fainting bride remember,
As a hart leap to her side;
Let not Amalek o'erthrow her
Utterly in warlike pride;
Prowling foxes wander through her,
Spoil her clusters day by day;
The Shekina of God's presence
Slowly, slowly draws away.

Lord, awake! display thy valour,
Thy great covenant maintain;
See thy name traduced and blackened
Where thy witnesses lie slain;
Thou who art the Resurrection,
Speak the word, and they shall rise,
Thy new name inscribed upon them,
Radiant as the morning skies.

Thy new name is precious ointment,
Fragrant, powerful and free,
Rendering foemen worthy objects
Of the love of One in Three;
For with God is no repentance;
None shall e'er his work delay
Till his sheaves lie in his bosom,
Gathered in, and safe for aye.

13.

I shall tread the Vale of Weeping
Till the blood divine is seen
Pouring from the Rock, a river
That has made ten thousand clean;
If his light
Pierce the night
I shall find my way aright.

I am longing for the moment
That shall all my right disclose —
Jesus, tree of life immortal,
Source whence all our justice flows;
Boldly there
I'll repair,
No more useless fig-leaves wear.

What have I to do henceforward
With vain idols of this earth?
Nothing can I find among them
To compete with his high worth.
Be my dwelling
In his love through all my days.

14.

> O wonder always, happy bride,
> To whom thou art in love allied;
> Ye ransomed seed, his wonders tell,
> Who o'er ten thousand doth excel.

15.

> There he stands among the myrtles,
> Worthiest object of my love;
> Yet in part I know his glory
> Towers all earthly things above;
> One glad morning
> I shall see him as he is.

> He's the beauteous Rose of Sharon,
> White and ruddy, fair to see;
> Excellent above ten thousand
> Of the world's prime glories he.
> Friend of sinners,
> He's their pilot on the deep.

16.

Earth cannot, with all its trinkets,
Slake my longings at this hour;
They were captured, they were widened,
When my Jesus showed his power.
None but he can now content me,
He, the Incomprehensible;
O to gaze upon his Person,
God in man made visible.

Let my days be wholly given
Jesus' blood to glorify,
Calm to rest beneath his shadow,
At his feet to live and die,
Love the cross, and bear it daily,
('Tis the cross my Husband bore,)
Gaze with joy upon his Person,
And unceasingly adore.

17.

Lapped in a sea of wonders
O might I spend my days,
Upon the Blood depending
The while I tread earth's ways,
And find my thoughts made captive
To Christ's authority,
And, with his law conforming,
His faithful witness be.

18.

God's table could provide no food,
While sin was reigning,
But shadows of a future good,
Our hope sustaining;
When came the day of Jubilee,
The veil was riven;
The law, in Jesus on the tree,
Saw justice given.

19.

>Let not any, for my blackness,
>Gaze upon me doubtingly;
>'Tis the sun that, high in splendour,
>Shoots his fiery shafts at me;
>Yet I'm covered —
>Solomon's curtains give me shade.

20.

>When the primal pair fell captive
>'Neath the law of sin and fate,
>God, the God of love, by nature
>Found himself compelled to hate;
>Yet though wrathful, still he loved them,
>Rescued them in their distress,
>Nothing bated of his justice,
>Perfect in his changelessness.

21.

O to pierce into the knowledge
Of the one, true, living Lord,
Slaying all imaginations,
Holding solely by the Word;
To believe what there stands written,
What from thence is clearly known: —
Sinners cannot live before him;
He, he only, must atone.

Where this truth is seen and pondered,
Lofty looks are overthrown;
Man is little, weak and loathsome,
God is great, and God alone;
Christ, our precious Mediator,
Can alone our state repair;
Guilty souls, his work beholding,
Worship God incarnate there.

22.

God, though infinite in mercy,
God of love although he be,
When I think on him, affrights me,
Troubles me, disquiets me;
Yet within the tent of meeting
Throned he sits as God of grace,
Peace and reconciliation
Gently radiant in his face.

There my food and drink are furnished,
There my rest and refuge are,
There my healing and my treasure,
There my stronghold in the war;
There I find my warlike harness,
Arming me to face the foe;
There my life is safely hidden
When to conflict forth I go.

God my Father, God my Refuge,
God my Stronghold, Rock and Tower —
More I cannot ask when round me
Fire and flood put forth their power;
He my every want supplying,
I'll repel an armed host;
Lacking him, I'm weak and strengthless,
And the day is truly lost.

23.

His left hand, in heat of noonday,
Lovingly my head upholds,
And his right hand, filled with blessings,
Tenderly my soul enfolds.
I adjure you, nature's darlings,
Beautiful in field and grove,
Stir not up, till he be willing,
Him who is my glorious Love.

24.

Wondrous sight for men and angels!
Wonders, wonders without end!
He who made, preserves, sustains us,
He our Ruler and our Friend,
Here lies cradled in the manger,
Finds no resting-place on earth,
Yet the shining hosts of glory
Throng to worship at his birth.

When thick cloud lies over Sinai,
And the trumpet's note rings high,
In Christ the Word I'll pass the barrier,
Climb, and feast, nor fear to die;
For in him all fullness dwelleth,
Fullness to restore our loss;
He stood forth and made atonement
Through his offering on the cross.

He between a pair of robbers
Hung, our Making-good to be;
He gave power to nerve and muscle
When they nailed him to the tree;
He, his Father's law exalting,
Paid our debt and quenched our flame;
Righteousness, in fiery splendour,
Freely pardons in his name.

See, my soul, where our Peace-maker,
King of kings, was lowly laid,
He, creation's life and movement,
Of the grave a tenant made,
Yet on souls fresh life bestowing;
Angels view it with amaze;
God in flesh with us adoring;
Heaven's full chorus shouts his praise.

Thanks for ever, thanks ten thousand,
While I've breath, all thanks and praise
To the God who all his wonders
For my worship here displays,
In my nature tried and tempted
Like the meanest of our race,
Man — a weak and helpless infant,
God — of matchless power and grace.

Gone this body of corruption,
'Mid the fiery hosts on high,
Gazing deep into the wonders
Wrought of old on Calvary,
God, the Invisible, beholding,
Him who lives, yet once was slain,
Clasped in close eternal union
And communion I'll remain.

There, new-fashioned in his likeness,
Veils and fancies done away,
To the Name by God exalted
Highest homage I shall pay.
There, communing in the secret
Seen in those deep wounds he bore,
I shall kiss the Son for ever,
Turning from him nevermore.

25.

Must I face the stormy river?
There is One to still the wave;
Jesus, my High Priest, is with me,
Strong to hold me, strong to save;
In his bosom I'll cry conquest,
(Death, and world, and hell defied,)
Lacking now all means of sinning,
In his likeness glorified.

Sweet to think upon the cov'nant
Made on high ere time began,
Gazing ever on the Person
Who assumed the form of man;
Unto death his soul was troubled,
All the agreement to fulfil;
Now the ransomed seven-score-thousand
Shout and sing on Zion's hill.

There no fiery sun at noonday
Smites; there death itself is slain;
Freed from sorrow, there the blessed
Sing of One in mortal pain;
There they swim in life's pure river
Flowing from the holy Three,
'Neath those peaceful rays unclouded
Streaming down from Calvary.

26.

God, make me like a tree well planted grow
In fertile ground where living waters flow,
Wide-rooting, ever green, and fruiting free
'Neath showers from that dire wound on Calvary.

God's promised land is good; it knows no woe;
In all its borders milk and honey flow;
Fine clusters thence are brought on desert ways;
A heavenly land, and none can speak its praise.

Jehovah he, and true to his great name;
His promises are true, his word the same;
He lifts his hand, forth comes a new-born race,
To all a proof of his free boundless grace.

27.

Must my zeal, that for the glory
Like a fiery coal once glowed,
And my youthful loving ardour,
Now wax colder towards my God?
Thou whose dwelling is high heaven,
Now thy matchless beauty show;
From the breasts of this creation
Wean my soul for ever now.

28.

When from Sinai's fiery summit
God of old proclaimed his law,
Sinners stood below, and trembled,
Fearing death from what they saw;
Yet they might, amid the thunder,
At his feet an altar see;
Offerings made on it foreshadowed
One great Offering yet to be.

29.

> Still the streams of our salvation,
> Filled with living virtue, flow,
> Free unfailing gifts of healing
> Ever ready to bestow;
> Suffers from the fall in Eden,
> Use these waters for your cure;
> Never-ending are the virtues
> Of Bethesda's substance pure.

30.

> I'll walk on softly day by day,
> The cross o'ershadowing all my way,
> And as I walk, my course I'll run,
> And I run I'll stand and see
> The full salvation that shall be
> When I'm no more beneath the sun.

31.

Lo, to us is born a brother,
Born for hard and troublous days,
Faithful, full of consolation,
Worthy of yet higher praise.
Freedom sealing, sickness healing.
Way to Zion straight and free,
Fount clear-flowing, life bestowing,
God our saving ark is he.

32.

Not the great wide-rolling oceans
E'er can hide man's sin away;
Not the mighty Flood could drown it,
It is living still today;
But the precious blood and merits
Of the Lamb that once was slain —
There's the ocean that can hide it;
It will ne'er be seen again.

33.

There is not on earth an object
That can bring content to me;
My sole pleasure, my sole comfort
Is thy glorious face to see;
This can break the bonds that bind me
To all creatures here below;
Friends and kinsfolk shrink to nothing
If but thy great name I know.

34.

Lord God, from whose deep counsels
Salvation had its birth,
Thou only art the ruler
Of all in heaven and earth;
In face of tribulation,
Whatever may betide,
Let thy strong grace assist me
Beneath thy hand to hide.

A Note on Further Reading

In English:

Homage to Ann Griffiths (Church in Wales Publications, 1976).
This contains a verse translation of the hymns and a notable
lecture on Ann by Saunders Lewis, together with an intro-
duction by H.A. Hodges.
John Ryan, ed., *The Hymns of Ann Griffiths* (Ty ar y Graig,
1980). The text in Welsh with a translation, and a critical in-
troduction.
A.M. Allchin, 'Ann Griffiths, Mystic and Theologian' in *The
Kingdom of Love and Knowledge* (Darton, Longman & Todd,
1979).
Tony Conran, *Welsh Verse Translations* (Poetry Wales Press,
1986).
Joseph Clancy, *Twentieth Century Welsh poems in Translation*
(Gomer Press, 1984).

In Welsh:

Sian Megan, ed., *Gwaith Ann Griffiths* (Christopher Davies,
1982). A critical edition of the hymns and letters, with a full
introduction.
Dyfnallt Morgan, ed., *Y Ferch o Dolwar Fach* (Gwasg
Gwynedd, 1977). Lectures given at the 1976 summer school
on Ann.
R.M. Jones, *Ann Griffiths, Y Cyfrinydd Sylweddol* (Llyfrgell
Efengylaidd Cymru, 1977). An essay on Ann's teaching by a
noted evangelical scholar.

INDEX

Cowley Publications is a work of the Society of St. John the Evangelist, a religious community for men in the Episcopal Church. The books we publish are a significant part of our ministry, together with the work of preaching, spiritual direction, and hospitality. Our aim is to provide books that will enrich their readers' religious experience as well as challenge it with fresh approaches to religious concerns.